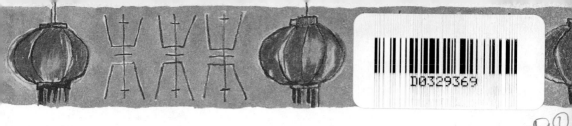

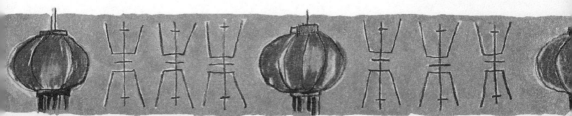

Classic
CHINESE
C·U·I·S·I·N·E

Edited by Rosemary Moon

SMITHMARK

ILLUSTRATIONS BY
CAMILLA SOPWITH AND ROD FERRING

CLB 4364
© 1995 CLB Publishing

This edition published in 1995 by Smithmark Publishers, Inc.
16 East 32nd Street, New York NY 10016

SMITHMARK books are available for bulk purchase for sales promotion
and premium use. For details write or call the manager of special sales,
SMITHMARK Publishers, Inc.
16 East 32nd Street, New York,
NY 10016; (212) 532-6600

Produced by CLB Publishing
Godalming Business Centre
Woolsack Way, Godalming, Surrey, UK

ISBN 0-8317-1178-7

Printed in South Africa
10 9 8 7 6 5 4 3 2 1

73-43760mm

CONTENTS

INTRODUCTION

China is an enormous place! It is the world's third largest country, with an area of almost 9.6 million square km or 3.7 million square miles, smaller only than Russia and Canada. It includes more than 3,400 off-shore islands, the largest of which, Hainan, in the South China Sea, is about the same size as Sardinia.

The Largest Population

China has the largest population in the world, with more than one–fifth of the total global population living within its borders. In such an enormous country is not at all surprising that geographical differences have resulted in strong regional identities and traditions, and that these are apparent in many aspects of daily life, including China's great cuisine.

Home of the World's Oldest Civilization

With a recorded history of 3,500 years, China is certainly one of the oldest, if not *the* oldest, of the world's civilizations. Zhonghua, the Chinese name for the country, literally means "central land," reflecting the ancient Chinese belief that the country was the center of the world and the only true civilization.

Ancient Chinese skills and technology matched those of the Romans, especially in their ability to make paper and to produce porcelain. These superior skills led the ancient people of China to cut themselves off from the rest of the world, regarding all others as barbarians. This had little detrimental effect on the country until the Industrial Revolution, by which time China had started to fall behind the other developed countries.

It was not until the Communists came to power in China in 1949 that programs for economic development and social change were introduced that have helped to transform China into a modern nation. Since the 1970s China has sought to return to the international community from its self-imposed isolation, and there is now far greater freedom for the exchange of information and for travel to and from this great country.

The Regions of China

China is divided into many regions for local government purposes, but for the explanation of Chinese cuisine four main areas illustrate the differing culinary tastes and traditions. These are the south, based around Canton; the north, where the cuisine includes many great banquet dishes as the Imperial Court of China at Beijing (Peking) was situated here; the east; and the west, which includes Szechuan province, home of much of China's hottest and spiciest food.

The geographical and economic differences between these areas contribute much to the basic differences between the foods. However, many dishes are common throughout China and it is the special foods that were traditionally cooked for banquets and celebrations that really underline the regional differences.

A Great Cuisine in the Tradition of France

The only other cuisine that I have studied that reveals the same

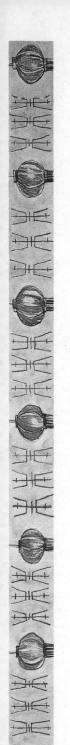

passion for cooking is that of France. France also has a wide variety of climates which are illustrated in its regional cookery. Any book that is to concentrate on French country cooking must divide, or at least research, the recipes by region. Should this also be the case for Chinese cooking? Well perhaps, but I have not done so, as I feel that those who are just beginning to enjoy Chinese cooking will want to look up recipes by the main ingredient and not by the area from which they come.

The purists in classical Chinese cooking, those who take their recipes from the vast selection that have been cooked and used in China for centuries, are skilled in the ancient ingredients and seasonings that make this a truly great cuisine. However, for those of us who are enthusiastic amateurs and newcomers to Chinese cooking, some of the dishes that we know best – which have led us to a thirst for greater knowledge of this cuisine – are in fact virtually unknown in China!

The Chinese Cooking of the West

In the nineteenth century many families emigrated from China to America and Europe. Some set up restaurants, sharing their culinary skills and knowledge with a public hungry for their "new" style of cooking. As time went on and Chinese restaurants became more and more popular, it was easy for customers to assume that the food they were served in the restaurants was indeed the classic cuisine of China. However, as is often the case, one has to adapt to survive and the restaurateurs introduced some dishes to their menus that would appeal to the Western palate and had a Chinese flavor but were not strictly classical Chinese recipes. Perhaps the most famous of these is chop suey, one of the most popular of all dishes on the restaurant menu outside China, yet relatively unknown inside the country, except by those who have had to leave their native shores to discover it! The ubiquitous serving of canned lychees and ice cream for dessert is another culinary "invention," and yet it must be popular to remain on so many menus.

The Best of Both Worlds

So, for this collection of classic Chinese recipes I have included some from the truly classical cooking of regional China, as well as some of the most popular dishes found in restaurants around the world. These may not strictly be classics, but they are popular standards through which many of us gain our initial enthusiasm for Chinese food and they deserve a place in both our affections and this book.

Southern China – a Land of Haute Cuisine

We are probably more familiar with Cantonese or southern Chinese cooking in the West than with any other regional style of Chinese cuisine. This is because the early émigrés who opened the first Chinese restaurants in the West were from this area. Cantonese cooking is widely regarded as the best in China, the haute cuisine amongst an eclectic culinary tradition which still manages to retain local characteristics. Much of the luxurious nature of celebratory Cantonese cooking is attributed to the chefs of the Imperial Court who fled south for refuge from Beijing when the Ming Dynasty was overthrown in the seventeenth century. These were the chefs who had the time to experiment with the snack foods, or dim sum, that are now such an established part of Chinese cuisine and enormously popular in the West.

Delicacy or Travesty?

One aspect of Cantonese cooking that is much frowned upon in the West is the tradition of experimenting with so-called delicacies or exotic foods. Regrettably these include (or certainly have in the past) such things as dog and turtle. In most countries the use of popular pets, dogs and cats, as food is very much frowned upon except perhaps in extreme emergencies. Turtles are now regarded as a species to be protected, hence more mock turtle soup is now sold than real. Turtles were on this earth before the dinosaurs and have survived much – we ought to be making efforts to keep them in existence rather than killing them unnecessarily for food.

Light Flavors and Seasonings

The cuisine of southern China explores the natural flavors of foods without the heavy seasoning of garlic, chilies and spices – although oyster sauce, which is made along the coast, is widely used here, as it is throughout China. All Chinese cooking is comparatively quick but the southern Chinese prefer their food slightly undercooked, even by Chinese standards. Thus

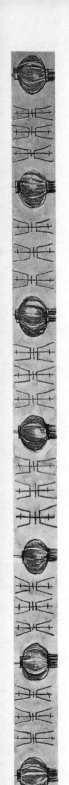

foods retain their color and texture, making both stir-frying and steaming popular methods of cooking. When cooking in the Cantonese way all your ingredients must be as fresh as possible and in prime condition.

The coastline of this region of China is over 1,000 miles long and provides a rich harvest of crabs, lobsters, oysters and other seafood, the shellfish being as highly prized in China as they are in northern Europe. The main difference in the preparation is that the Chinese are used to cooking their shellfish themselves, ensuring that it is as fresh as possible. Very few people in the West would go to this trouble, although it is now possible to buy raw shrimp in most large supermarkets and their flavor is definitely superior to those cooked prior to freezing.

The Rice Bowl of China

Southern China is one of the major rice-growing areas, earning the region the colloquial name of the rice bowl of China. This term is also applied to the western region, another rice–growing area. The cooking of rice is an art, and one of great importance in a cuisine where it is a staple part of the diet. Rice is used for both savory and sweet dishes, although the former are far more popular in China.

Rice is also ground into flour and used for noodles, which are popular throughout China. It is the basic Chinese breakfast as well, in the form of congee, a porridge-like concoction of soft, watery rice.

Northern China – Home of the Imperial Court

The cooking of northern China is perhaps the next most elaborate after that of the south. Very different in climate from the area around Canton, the north includes the ancient capital of China, Beijing. It is too cold in the north to cultivate rice and so the staple foods are grains, including wheat and millet. These are often ground into flour and then made into pancakes and dumplings.

Peking Duck – a True Classic?

Well, I would have to say that the answer to that question is no. A modern-day classic perhaps, but not an ancient recipe, handed down through countless generations. However, it is probably the most famous of all Chinese dishes and a great favorite around the world. It is always served with a spicy plum sauce, shredded cucumber and scallions and pancakes but never with rice. Perhaps it has achieved such popularity outside China because it is eaten wrapped in pancakes? This, however, is a regional means to an end and not a culinary garnish – Peking Duck could not be served with rice, which is seldom eaten in the north, whereas pancakes are a staple food.

Another reason why Peking Duck cannot be considered to be an ancient classic dish of China is that very few homes, or indeed restaurants, have ovens and the duck for this recipe is always roasted. More of this later!

Three Great Influences

The cooking of northern China, and especially of the area around Beijing, has developed under three influences: the Chinese Moslems, the cooking of the Imperial Place and the peasant cooking of the area.

When Genghis Khan captured Beijing in the thirteenth century he brought with him many of the traditions of the western provinces of China, where large animals, such as cattle, deer, pigs and sheep were common and spit-roasting was widely used to cook the meat. Some people feel that this was an early influence on the creation of Peking Duck, and perhaps it was.

It is argued that the Imperial Palace influenced the cooking of this region less than the Moslems and the local peasant cooking because the last Emperors of China were from Manchuria, an area which has few, if any, specific dishes to call its own. The Manchu or Ch'ing Dynasty actually lasted from 1644 to 1912 and saw the times of greatest stability in China as well as a dramatic decline in the economy and total mismanagement of resources. However, it also saw a marked increase of interest in food in the Imperial Household and – after Emperor Ch'ien-lung visited Canton, tasting the cuisine of the south of his great country – steps were taken to introduce recipes from the south to the north, especially into the Imperial Household. These eventually influenced the whole cuisine of the region.

The country or peasant cooking of the area contributes the noodle and dumpling or "steamed bun" recipes to the cuisine

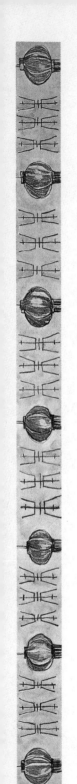

of northern China. In the harsher and more extreme climate ways had to be found to preserve vegetables for use throughout the winter, and dried mushrooms, pickled fruits and vegetables, and smoked and dried meats are all common in this area. Fresh vegetables which store well, like turnips and onions, are also widely used, as are garlic, scallions and leeks. Confucius was from the northern region of China and probably had a few wise thoughts on the cuisine of the area!

The Land-locked West

The western region is not only without any sea coast, it is also virtually cut off from the rest of China by mountains. The area includes the Szechuan and Hunan regions and Szechuan cooking is becoming very popular in the West, with its hot, spicy flavors derived from chilies, pickles and other seasonings. Szechuan peppercorns, much used in this area, are hot and distinctive and should be sought out for Chinese cooking.

Szechuan is situated in the fertile valley of the upper reaches of the Yangtze River which, at 5,520 km (3,430 miles) long, is the longest river in Asia and the fifth longest in the world. The Yangtze actually has the largest, most populated and the most fertile valley of all the great rivers and has been renowned for its fertility for at least 2,000 years. Hunan is similar to Szechuan in that it too is situated in a river basin, that of the Han, a tributary of the Yangtze. Both regions enjoy the same climate, one of hot, sultry summers and relatively mild winters. People of the world's hotter climates often enjoy a hot and spicy diet and the western Chinese follow suit, using copious amounts of garlic, onions and ginger in conjunction with red chilies.

A Feudal Flavor

In this fertile and productive area of China there has always been a flourishing agriculture and plentiful fruits and vegetables. Pork is popular, as are poultry and fish, although the region relies on rivers for fish as it has no sea coast. The vast areas of land to be worked have led to a feudal approach to life in this part of China, with workers or peasants and landlords, all of whom were ruled by warlords. The cooking of the area very much reflects these social differences with the majority of food being plainer, usually steamed, and yet still fiery in flavor, using all the local seasonings. The warlords and some of the landlords enjoyed a more elaborate style of eating, combining more flavors into each dish and usually toning down the robustness of the hot pepper seasonings. These upmarket dishes were rather more like the cooking of the north, but retained the regional ingredients and flavors of the western provinces.

Fu-Yung, a Favorite in Szechuan

Fu-yung, a popular dish based originally on egg whites and not the whole egg, is perhaps a surprisingly mild dish to be a favorite in this region of highly spiced foods, but popular it is. Many people now refer to any dish that includes eggs as a fu-yung, whereas in terms of classical Chinese cuisine it should indicate only the whites of eggs, mixed with cornstarch and ground chicken and then fried. Stock might be added to the fried chicken to make a sauce to serve with vegetables or other rather bland dishes to give more flavor. Any vegetable can be prepared in this way, making cauliflower, carrot, cabbage or whatever fu-yung. The secret of preparing the dish well is to poach or steam the vegetables until soft before quickly stir-frying them with the fu-yung to finish the dish without overcooking and toughening the eggs.

The Eastern Region

Last but not by any means least amongst the culinary regions of China is the eastern region. This area stretches inland to central China from the east coast and includes the largest city and busiest port in the country, Shanghai. The lower valley of the River Yangtze provides a wonderfully fertile river plain and this area, where many fresh fruits and vegetables are grown, is particularly noted for its vegetarian dishes. The Yangtze and the coastline ensure plentiful supplies of fish throughout the region; indeed, there seems to be plenty of everything here.

A Land of Plenty

The great abundance of food allows for all sorts of culinary experimentation and there are many excellent restaurants of international repute in and around Shanghai. Vegetarianism is more popular amongst those who are better off and can afford to pick and choose their food. In the eastern region, where all foods are plentiful, there is sufficient choice to make an interesting meatless diet.

The Best Ingredients and the Lightest of Sauces

With so many ingredients available in absolutely first class condition, eastern cooking tends to be light, and the sauces and seasonings added to food are mild so as not to mask the natural flavors of the prime quality ingredients. Steaming is a very popular method of cooking and great lengths are taken to accentuate the flavor of the principal ingredient of each dish. Soy sauce, the most popular of all Chinese seasonings, is produced here; indeed the best soy sauce in all China is produced in the eastern region, as is the best vinegar, Chingkiang, used both as a seasoning and a dipping sauce.

Sugar, Adding Sweetness and Richness

Sugar grows well in the eastern region and the people of this area are said to have a sweet tooth! They certainly use sugar in many of their recipes, and add it to savory dishes to accentuate flavors – it is often used with fish, meat, shellfish and vegetables. There can be no doubt that a little sugar added to a Western beef casserole at the end of the cooking adds richness and a roundness of flavor – well, the same applies here and, when combined with the use of oil, sugar has earned the area a reputation for rich and lavish food.

Vegetable and Fried Rices

The eastern region certainly grows a good crop of rice, the area's staple food. In many other regions rice is almost always boiled or steamed but in the east there has been much experimentation, leading to numerous dishes of fried vegetable rice. These might include just one vegetable, stir-fried to release its flavor, and then added to the rice during boiling or steaming. The vegetable, whether onion, leek or something more exotic, then flavors the rice during the cooking process.

Fried rices have become especially popular with Western enthusiasts for Chinese cooking. Perhaps this is because boiled rice can become a little dull and relies upon the food that it accompanies. In China fried rice is a snack, a complete meal in itself, which explains why there are often many ingredients in what is otherwise a staple food. It would never be served in a traditional meal setting, being too flavorsome and complex to accompany other dishes. When eaten in restaurants outside China, fried rice requires only one dish to accompany it to provide a satisfying meal.

Eating in the Chinese Way

Eating Chinese food in the traditional way is a very distinctive experience. In the United States, we would expect to begin a

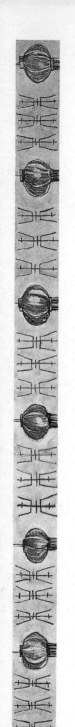

formal meal with an appetizer, perhaps a soup, followed by a main course and a dessert – with some cheese, either before or after the pudding, if the meal is to be a little more lavish.

Chinese meals are not served in this way, except at grand parties and formal banquets. For everyday eating and home entertaining a selection of dishes are prepared for the meal, but they are all laid out as a spread and served more or less simultaneously, with soups (usually one or two) served more as drinks than as appetizers. Dim sum, either sweet or savory snacks, might be included in the meal, almost as punctuation marks, to refresh the palate at various stages, but this is more common at parties or banquets. Wine is seldom served and neither, surprisingly, is tea, except at banquets; the Chinese rely on their soups as drinks, which is why most varieties are little more than flavored or garnished stocks.

A typical family meal would usually consist of one or two soups and four or five main dishes, all chosen to provide contrast in colour and texture and a variety of fish, meat and poultry. Most Chinese main courses include some vegetables but a separate vegetable dish might also be served, along with the staple of the area – rice, wheat or millet, pancakes or dumplings.

Desserts – a Special Treat

Desserts are seldom served except on special occasions, at parties or at banquets. There are comparatively few classic dessert dishes and the best known of the limited selection is Eight Jewel or Eight Treasure Rice (see page 243), a lavish molded pudding revered in the same way as the Western Christmas Pudding. What few desserts the Chinese do have don't really measure up to Western notions, and in most cases, both in China and abroad, the best way to finish a Chinese meal is with a lusciously ripe piece of fresh fruit.

The Chinese do, however, have a tradition of sweet dim sum, little mouthfuls of delicious petit-four-like creations, which are served in tea houses. These are popular with Chinese and Westerners alike, and dim sum, both sweet and savory, are often served in cafés in Hong Kong where it is not uncommon to find people making a complete meal out of 10 or 12 different varieties of these snacks.

Banquets and Big Occasions

Chinese people never have to look very far to find an excuse for a party. Food on these occasions is of prime importance and is served in a slightly different way to a family meal. Indeed, a banquet is served in a similar style to a formal Western meal.

Guests at a banquet might expect a selection of cold dishes to be served on arrival, in a similar manner to anti-pasta at the start of an Italian meal. The next selection of dishes is usually hot, dry fried foods, almost like warm cocktail savories. Wine will be served throughout a banquet.

The meal then progresses with a vast selection of dishes being presented to guests in small groups, allowing them time to savor each "course" as it is presented hot and freshly cooked. Many meats and a selection of fish dishes will be included and perhaps as many as four or five different dishes of rice. In the north, where grains and dumplings are more common than rice, the heavier foods such as dumplings will be reserved for the end of the meal, so that guests might enjoy a wide variety of dishes without getting full too early on!

Desserts will be served with a selection of the wonderful fruits grown in China, both fresh and preserved.

Well, I feel full just having written about that! I will add that it was common to serve around 60 dishes at a banquet and at the grandest of all occasions, the All-China Manchu Banquet, around 300 were served! Such lavish entertaining is now less common, despite the fact that the Chinese are still passionate and most particular about their food, enjoying every opportunity that presents itself to show hospitality and to share good fortune. Things are being scaled down gradually to more sensible-size celebrations, with less waste and extravagance.

The Ancient Center of Vegetarianism

Vegetarianism is not new, it has been practised for many hundreds of years by certain sects of the Buddhist faith and much of the tradition of a meatless diet stems from the Buddhist monasteries of China. I first came across lo-han vegetables at our local Chinese restaurant and they are delicious – the lo-hans are minor gods of the Buddhist faith. Vegetables cooked in this style are served in a light but savory gravy and have a delightfully fresh fragrance. Single vegetables or a mixture of two or three, or vegetables mixed with tofu or bean curd for

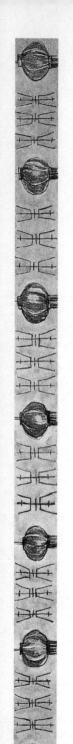

extra protein, are delicious when prepared in the style of the lo-hans.

A Very Healthy Diet

Very few Chinese, even today, have ovens, which means that the vast majority of Chinese dishes are cooked over an open fire or on a burner. The cooking methods are simple and the most popular are steaming and stir-frying. Most dishes are cooked quickly in just one pot or wok and are simple to assemble – it is not surprising that woks are popular today among the students of the West!

Stir-frying is a healthy way to cook. Only the minimum amount of oil is required and the food is cooked quickly, retaining many of its vitamins and minerals. It is very interesting to compare the following average daily intake of calories in the West with a typical Chinese diet:

	N. America	W. Europe	China
Daily intake	3,170 calories	3,050 calories	2,060 calories
Protein	11.9%	11.3%	11.6%
Fat	41.5%	35.8%	13.7%
Carbohydrate	46.6%	52.9%	74.7%

It simply cannot be healthy for Americans to eat over three times as much fat as the Chinese and for Europeans to eat over two and a half times as much.

Special Ingredients for a Special Cuisine

There are many ingredients that are essential to good Chinese cooking which were virtually unheard of in the average Western household until a few years ago. I suppose that we have known about soy sauce since Chinese restaurants first became popular, but not everyone knows that there are light and dark varieties.

Some of the more unusual ingredients are still hard to find unless you have a Chinese supermarket close by, but these are common in major towns and cities. Large supermarkets also stock a fair selection of canned vegetables and fresh herbs suitable for Chinese and Oriental cooking, as well as basic stir-fry sauces. However, "Chinese-flavored" food is becoming more and more popular, and many varieties of sauces and ingredients are being produced with exotic sounding names. These are not all strictly correct for Chinese cuisine; and for some the instructions are incorrect. For example, I recently bought some fine rice noodles which were recommended for adding to stir-fries but would have been much better used for adding substance to a soup, which is how the Chinese would use them.

What is It?

To help you through the maze of exotic ingredients called for in some of the following recipes here is a brief run-down of what is what:

Soy Sauce A basic seasoning sauce which has a salty flavor and is used instead of salt in most Chinese cooking. It is made from a mixture of soy beans, flour and water which is naturally fermented and then matured. The best soy sauce comes from the area around Shanghai. Of the two types of soy sauce, light soy is the saltier and is best for general cooking, whereas the dark is matured for longer and is more suitable for rich meat dishes and stews.

Black Beans Chinese black beans are not to be confused with the small black kidney beans of South America. They are soy beans fermented with salt and spices and are usually sold canned outside China. Rinse the beans in cold water before use. Any left-over beans can be stored in a sealed container in the refrigerator for many weeks.

Chinese Mushrooms Many varieties of mushrooms are used in Chinese cooking, both fresh and dried. Outside China most of the mushrooms are dried – they look rather strange but do have a wonderful flavor. It may not be possible to obtain all the varieties called for in the following recipes unless you have a specialist Chinese supermarket or shop nearby. The mushrooms will keep for a long time so look out for them when you have the opportunity. Straw mushrooms are only available in cans and should be rinsed in cold water before use.

Szechuan Preserved or Pickled Vegetables This is a pickled vegetable root, preserved in salt and hot chilies. It is hot and crunchy and is an unusual and pungent addition to many Szechuan dishes. The pickles should be rinsed and chopped before use. If they are not available, I would suggest using a hot Indian-style relish – it will not be the same and purists will throw up their hands in horror, but it will introduce some fire to your cooking.

Spring Roll & Wonton Skins These papers, skins or wrappers are very thin and rather difficult to make at home. Make life a little easier for yourself and buy fresh or frozen wrappers from a specialist Chinese shop.

Sugar Chinese sugar is processed differently from that available in the West. For most accurate results use granulated sugar – either white or light brown.

Rice Wine This is rich and mellow and is made from glutinous rice and spring water, fermented with a little yeast. A good quality pale dry sherry is the closest alternative but the Chinese would consider it to be a poor substitute for rice wine.

Oils Groundnut or peanut oil is the best to use for Chinese cooking, although corn and vegetable oils also work well. The very fragrant sesame oil is seldom used for cooking by the Chinese but is added as an extra seasoning at the last moment to prepared dishes.

Bean Curd, Doufu, or Tofu Tofu is actually the Japanese name for bean curd but it is the name by which it is mostly widely known in the West. It is a solidified paste made from ground yellow soy beans. There are two varieties available in most supermarkets, a solid variety for stir-fries and most general cooking, and a smoother silken tofu which is softer and therefore more suitable for soups. Silken tofu is generally a long-life product and may be found on the supermarket shelves, whereas the fresh blocks of solid tofu will be found in the refrigerated cabinets. Tofu is more of a texture than a taste but is widely used in Chinese cooking and is valued in vegetarian cooking all over the world as a very rich source of vegetable protein.

These are the basics of the Chinese larder. Other ingredients are discussed in individual recipes. As interest in all types of

cooking continues to grow, it is becoming increasingly easy to obtain the ingredients with which to make authentic Chinese food.

The Versatile Wok

All you need now before you can start cooking in the Chinese way is a wok! Of course you can use a skillet, but a wok is better. It is designed in such a way that only a small surface area is actually in contact with the heat. Once food is cooked it can be drawn up the sides of the wok to keep warm while preventing overcooking, leaving the hottest area ready for the next ingredient to be added. This cannot be done in a skillet, so exactly the same results cannot be achieved as in a wok.

Woks need not be expensive, indeed the best ones are often made from relatively thin gauge metal that conducts heat easily and rapidly. Electric woks and cast-iron woks have been introduced in the West, but neither would receive rave reviews in China! Buy a wok with a lid and a trivet so that it can also be used as a steamer. Seasoned well with oil when new, according to the instructions supplied with it, your wok should last for years.

The Art of Using Chopsticks

Well, I'll just give you a little tip – keep the lower stick firmly clasped and move the top one; well, that's how it works for me! Good luck!

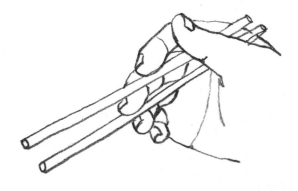

Soups

Soup formed the major part of many diets for centuries, when cooking techniques were limited and the equipment available was often just one pot over an open fire. In many of the great cuisines of the world it is almost possible to trace the development of a race through their soups. We can see how prosperity and an ever increasing range of both cooking equipment and ingredients led to soups becoming less substantial, a less important part of the meal, eventually becoming light and of infinite variety, to be served hot or cold, and usually as an appetizer.

Very little in China changed for thousands of years. Life in the country simply carried on and traditions in the home remained virtually unchanged, so it is reasonable to assume that many of the soups that are eaten in China today have been popular for many, many years.

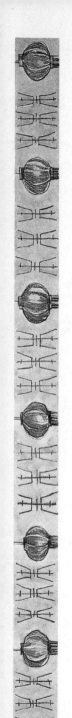

Soup as a Drink

It is quite usual to have two or more varieties of soup within the course of a typical Chinese meal. Soup is not eaten as a first course, an appetizer to whet your appetite, but as a part of a running buffet-style of meal. Many Chinese regard a bowl of soup as we would a glass of wine, to be dipped into when the palate is dry whilst feasting on other meat, fish or poultry dishes. This is why the vast majority of Chinese soups are what we would call "thin" or clear soups, often little more than a well-flavored stock with a vegetable or pasta garnish. These thin soups are easier to drink. Wine, water and tea are not traditionally served in China to accompany a family meal.

Thick Soups for Special Occasions

Anyone used to dining in Chinese restaurants in the West might reasonably assume that Crab & Sweetcorn, Chicken & Sweetcorn – and any other of the numerous soups thickened with this starchy vegetable – are truly classic Chinese dishes. Well, they may be old Chinese recipes but they are not considered to be such classics as the many varieties of clear soups. However, there are some highly prized thicker soups which are often part of a banquet or celebratory meal, when the soup is served in the Western style, before main meat, fish and poultry dishes.

Of all the thick soups the most special treat for the Chinese gourmet is Shark's Fin Soup. Shark's fin is a great delicacy and, even in China, it is expensive. The fin itself has comparatively little flavor – what it adds to the soup is the texture that makes this dish so special. The fin is sold dried and has to be soaked, preferably overnight, before use.

Good Stock – Good Soup

The secret of a good Chinese soup is exactly the same as that of any other soup from any other country in the world – a good stock! As many of the thin soups are little more than stock with garnish it is easy to see that a depth of flavor is vital if the soup is to be enjoyed.

As many Chinese dishes require meat, poultry or game there is never any shortage of bones and trimmings for making stock. Do not throw the bones away after preparing a dish of duck –

boil them up with a few fresh vegetables to make a rich and versatile stock. However, care should be taken when making game stock as it can become a little "gluey" or musty in flavor – this is easily rectified by adding some chicken bones to the stockpot.

Never cover the pan when making stock – this affects the flavor and can also make the stock cloudy, which would be disastrous for a Chinese clear soup. Add plenty of herbs and peppercorns for flavoring but do not season the stock with salt until it has been strained and reduced, otherwise the resulting liquor may be over-flavored.

Stock freezes very well. After preparing a pan of stock reserve some for immediate use – it will keep for about five days in the refrigerator if it has been prepared from fresh bones. Boil the remaining stock until well reduced and freeze it in small, usable quantities – preferably in blocks; it then takes up less room in the freezer. Add extra water, wine or sherry to the defrosted stock before using.

PEKING SLICED LAMB WITH CUCUMBER SOUP

Most Chinese soups are "thin" or clear soups, based on a good homemade stock. This soup is a little more substantial than most as it includes very finely sliced lamb fillet. Boneless lamb leg could also be used.

Serves 4-6

INGREDIENTS
½ pound lamb neck fillet
1 tbsp soy sauce
1½ tsps sesame oil
Half a cucumber
5 cups chicken stock
Salt and freshly ground black
  pepper
1½ tbsps wine vinegar

Cut the lamb into wafer thin slices, then sprinkle with the soy sauce and sesame oil. Marinate for 15 minutes. Slice the cucumber thinly.

Season the stock with salt and pepper, and bring to a boil. Add the sliced lamb and poach it in the stock for 2 minutes. Remove the meat with a slotted spoon. Poach the cucumber in the stock for 1 minute. Return the lamb, stir in the vinegar, adjust the seasoning and serve.

HOT & SOUR SOUP

Hot & Sour Soup has a sharp, peppery flavor which is most unusual. Although more traditional in Thai and Vietnamese cooking, a little very finely chopped lemon grass may be added.

Serves 4

INGREDIENTS
4 Chinese dried mushrooms
¼ lb lean pork fillet
2 tbsps sunflower or vegetable oil
¼ cup bamboo shoots, sliced
5 cups light, clear stock *or* hot water plus 2 chicken bouillon cubes
½ cup diced tofu or bean curd
1 tsp cornstarch
2 tbsps cold water
1 tsp sesame oil

Marinade
1 tbsp light soy sauce
3 tbsps vinegar
2 tbsps water
1 tsp sesame oil
Salt and freshly ground black pepper

Garnish
Fresh cilantro leaves

Soak the Chinese mushrooms for 20 minutes in hot water. Meanwhile, slice the pork fillet into thin slivers. Make the marinade by combining all the ingredients together, then pour it over the pork in a bowl, and leave for 30 minutes.

Drain the mushrooms, discard the stalks and slice the caps very finely. Remove the pork from the marinade with a slotted spoon and reserve the marinade.

Heat a wok, and add the sunflower or vegetable oil. When hot, add the pork, mushrooms and bamboo shoots and stir-fry for 2 minutes. Add the stock and bring to a boil, then simmer for 10 minutes. Add the bean curd, the marinade, and salt and pepper to taste. Mix the cornstarch to a paste with the cold water, then add it to the soup and let it simmer for 5 minutes. Add the sesame oil and sprinkle with fresh cilantro. Serve hot.

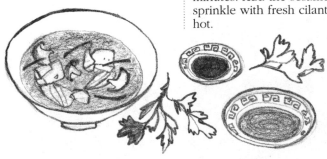

CHINESE COMBINATION SOUP

This soup combines many favorite soup ingredients in one broth – Chinese mushrooms, shredded chicken, noodles and vegetables – making a much heartier soup than most.

Serves 4

INGREDIENTS
4 Chinese dried mushrooms
¼ pound fine thread egg noodles
½ pound chicken
1 tbsp peanut oil
1 clove garlic, thinly sliced
1 tsp finely chopped fresh root
  ginger
2 shallots, finely sliced
1 cup shredded cabbage
2½ cups chicken stock
2 eggs, lightly beaten
1 tsp cornstarch
1 tbsp water
1 tbsp dark soy sauce
1 tbsp sherry

Soak the mushrooms in hot water for 20 minutes. Remove and discard the stalks, then slice the mushroom caps thinly. Soak the noodles in boiling salted water for 2 minutes, then rinse in cold water and drain. Slice the chicken finely.

Heat a wok and add the peanut oil. Add the garlic and ginger, and fry gently for 5 minutes, then discard the vegetables – they are used to flavor the oil. Add the chicken and fry for a few minutes until the meat has turned white. Add the mushrooms, shallots, cabbage and the stock. Bring to a boil, then simmer for 5 minutes. Gradually pour in the eggs and stir so that they cook in shreds. Mix the cornstarch to a paste with the water, and pour into the soup, stirring continuously. Cook for 2 minutes or until the soup boils and thickens. Add the noodles, soy sauce and sherry. Serve immediately.

FISH & RICE SOUP

The fish fillets used for this soup are cut into very fine shreds and need very litttle cooking. Letting them stand in the hot soup provides all the cooking that is necessary.

Serves 4

INGREDIENTS
3 cups fish stock
1 tbsp soy sauce
1 slice fresh root ginger, peeled and finely chopped
¾ pound fresh cod or haddock fillet
½ tsp cornstarch, combined with a little water
½ cup rice, part-cooked for 8 minutes
Salt and freshly ground black pepper

Heat the fish stock, soy sauce and ginger together in a large pan. Cut the fish fillets into very thin slices and then into strips. Stir the cornstarch paste into the stock and simmer gently for 10 minutes, then add the drained, part-cooked rice. Cook for a further 5 minutes. Remove the pan from the heat and add the fish. Let the fish cook for 2-3 minutes in the hot soup. Check the seasoning, adding salt and pepper as necessary. Serve immediately.

DUCK SOUP

This soup is sometimes served after a main course of Peking Duck – it is made from the bones and one or two simple ingredients.

Serves 4

INGREDIENTS
½ Chinese cabbage
2 cups diced tofu or bean curd
Bones of 1 duck
2 tbsps soy sauce
1 tbsp vinegar
5 cups water

Cut the cabbage into 2-inch pieces. Place the duck bones in a large pan with the cabbage, bean curd, soy sauce and vinegar. Add enough cold water to cover, and bring to a boil. Simmer the soup for 30 minutes, then remove the bones and serve the soup.

SHARK'S FIN SOUP

*Shark's fin is a highly prized delicacy in Chinese cooking. It
is the dorsal fin of certain species of shark which is salted
and then dried. This recipe uses crab and chicken for flavor
– the shark's fin merely adds texture to the soup.*

Serves 4-6

INGREDIENTS

2 ounces shark's fin
8 Chinese dried mushrooms
5 cups water
3-4 slices fresh root ginger,
    peeled
5 cups chicken stock
1 tsp salt
1 tbsp dark soy sauce
1 cup cooked crab
1½ cups shredded cooked
    chicken
2 tbsps cornstarch, blended with
    ⅓ cup water
3-4 tsps sesame oil

Soak the shark's fin and the dried mushrooms overnight in separate bowls of cold water. Drain the fins, then place them in a saucepan with the cold water. Shred the root ginger finely and add it to the pan. Bring to a boil, then simmer for 1½ hours. Drain and simmer in fresh water for a further 45 minutes, then drain again.

Drain the mushrooms, remove the stems and quarter the caps. Heat the stock in a saucepan or flameproof ceramic pot (the traditional Chinese utensil). When boiling, add the mushrooms and fins and simmer for 15 minutes. Add the salt, soy sauce and the crab. Bring to a boil and boil for 2-3 minutes. Add the shredded chicken and cornstarch mixture. Return the soup to a boil for a further 3-4 minutes. Sprinkle with sesame oil and serve.

WONTON SOUP WITH WATERCRESS

Wontons are often served fried but they are just as good boiled or steamed, when they may be served in soup. Be sure to seal the edges of the wonton wrappers to enclose the filling completely.

Serves 4-6

INGREDIENTS
1 bunch watercress
½ pound ground pork
2 tbsps soy sauce
2 tsps sesame oil
½ tsp sugar
1 tbsp white wine
½ tsp freshly ground black pepper
½ tsp ground ginger
¼ pound ready-made wonton wrappers
5 cups chicken stock
1 tsp salt

Chop half the watercress and place it in individual soup bowls. Rinse the other half in boiling water. Drain and chop finely, then mix it with the ground pork, 1 tbsp of the soy sauce, 1 tsp of the sesame oil, the sugar, white wine, pepper and ground ginger. Marinate for 5-6 minutes.

Place half a teaspoonful of mixture just below the center of each wonton wrapper. Fold one side over the filling. Moisten the corners with water and fold over to seal, completely enclosing the filling. Continue making wontons until all the filling mixture is used.

Bring 10 cups water to a boil in a deep pan, add the wontons, return to a boil and cook for 5 minutes. Bring the chicken stock to a boil in a separate pan, and add salt and the remaining soy sauce. Transfer the wontons to the soup, add the remaining sesame oil and pour the soup into the watercress-lined bowls.

FISH SOUP WITH SWEETCORN

This soup may seem extravagant as the mixed fish is discarded after preparing the stock. Fish heads and bones will make a good cheap stock if you are able to buy them.

Serves 4

INGREDIENTS
1 tbsp oil
1 carrot, chopped
1 onion, chopped
½ leek, chopped
1 bay leaf
2¼ pounds mixed fish
2 trout fillets
1 cod or fresh haddock fillet
2 tbsps oyster sauce
1 tbsp soy sauce
½ tsp cornstarch, combined with
   a little water
2 cups sweetcorn
Salt and freshly ground black
   pepper

To prepare a fish stock, heat the oil in a large saucepan and gently fry the carrot, onion, leek and bay leaf. When the vegetables are lightly colored, add the mixed fish, together with all the heads and bones. Cover with water and boil for 20 minutes. Pour through a fine strainer, keeping the stock only.

Slice the trout and cod or haddock fillets thinly and set them aside. Measure 3 cups of fish stock into a saucepan and bring it to a boil. Stir in the oyster sauce, soy sauce, cornstarch and sweetcorn, then boil for 10 minutes. Add the sliced fish and remove the pan from the heat. Check the seasoning, adding salt and pepper as necessary. Let stand for 1 minute before serving.

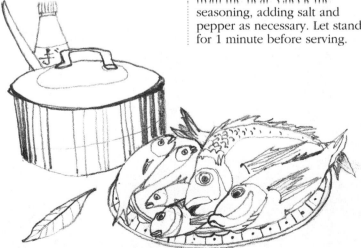

PEKING-STYLE SOUP

Duck stock is widely used in Chinese cooking as a large number of duck dishes are eaten, providing plenty of bones for stock. A brown chicken stock could be used as an alternative.

Serves 4

INGREDIENTS
4 slices smoked ham
3 cups shredded Bok Choy
3 cups duck stock
1 tbsp sesame seeds
1 small clove garlic, finely
   chopped
1 tbsp soy sauce
½ tsp white wine vinegar
Salt and freshly ground black
   pepper
1 egg yolk, beaten

Cut the ham into small, even-size pieces. Simmer the Bok Choy briskly for 10 minutes in the duck stock. Stir in the sesame seeds, garlic, ham, soy sauce and vinegar, and add salt and pepper to taste. Cook for 10 minutes over gentle heat. Using a teaspoon, trickle the beaten egg yolk into the soup. Serve immediately.

LAMB & NOODLE SOUP

*Use lamb neck fillet, thinly sliced, for this recipe. It is very
lean and tender and so it will cook quickly in this soup.*

Serves 4

INGREDIENTS
¼ pound cellophane noodles
6 Chinese dried mushrooms,
    soaked for 15 minutes in warm
    water
3 cups lamb stock, skimmed
⅓ pound lamb fillet, thinly sliced
1 tbsp soy sauce
¼ tsp chili sauce
Salt and freshly ground black
    pepper

Break the cellophane noodles
into small pieces and cook them
in boiling salted water for 20
seconds. Rinse them in fresh
water and set aside to drain.
Cook the mushrooms in lightly
salted boiling water for 15
minutes, then rinse them in fresh
water and set aside to drain. Cut
the mushrooms into thin slices.

Heat the lamb stock in a
saucepan and add the lamb,
mushrooms, soy sauce and chili
sauce. Season with salt and
pepper and simmer gently for 15
minutes. Stir in the drained
noodles and simmer for just long
enough to heat the noodles
through. Serve immediately.

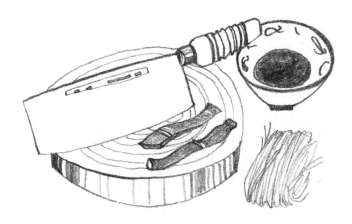

BAMBOO SHOOT SOUP

This is an elegant soup, elegant in flavor and in presentation. The strands of egg provide a very decorative garnish.

Serves 4

INGREDIENTS
½ cup bamboo shoots, cut into
 thin matchsticks
4 Chinese dried black
 mushrooms, soaked for 15
 minutes in warm water
3 cups chicken stock
1 tbsp wine vinegar
2 tbsps light soy sauce
Salt and freshly ground black
 pepper
½ tsp cornstarch, combined with
 a little water
1 egg, beaten
10 chives, chopped

Blanch the bamboo shoots in boiling, salted water for 3 minutes. Rinse and set aside to drain. Cook the mushrooms in boiling, salted water for 10 minutes. Rinse and set aside to drain.

Bring the stock to a boil in a large saucepan and add the bamboo shoots, mushrooms, vinegar and soy sauce. Season with salt and pepper to taste. Cook for 10 minutes. Stir in the cornstarch paste and bring the soup slowly back to a boil, then lower the heat. Place the beaten egg in a strainer and add to the soup by shaking the strainer back and forth over the hot soup – the egg will set in strands almost immediately. Add the chives to the soup and serve very hot.

CLEAR CHICKEN SOUP WITH EGG

Do not overcook the eggs when poaching or they will be tough and rubbery in the soup. Use a good homemade chicken stock in this soup for the very best results.

Serves 4

INGREDIENTS

4 Chinese dried mushrooms, soaked for 15 minutes in warm water
1 tbsp coarse sea salt
1 tbsp wine vinegar
1 bay leaf
4 eggs
3 cups chicken stock
1 onion, chopped
Salt and freshly ground black pepper
10 chives, chopped
1 tbsp soy sauce
¼ tsp chili sauce

Cook the mushrooms in boiling, salted water for 15 minutes. Rinse in fresh water and set aside to drain. Discard any hard stalks and cut the caps into thin slices. Bring a large saucepan of water to a boil with the sea salt, vinegar and bay leaf. Lower the heat to a gentle simmer and carefully break the eggs into the water one at a time. Poach the eggs for 1 minute and then remove them from the boiling water with a slotted spoon. Drain the eggs on a clean dish cloth.

Bring the stock to a boil in a saucepan with the onion, then simmer for 10 minutes. Pour through a fine strainer, discarding the onion. Check the seasoning, adding salt and pepper as necessary. Bring the stock back to a boil and add the mushrooms, chives, soy sauce and chili sauce. Cook for 10 minutes. One minute before serving, add the eggs.

FISH SOUP WITH SURPRISE WONTONS

This soup is lightly flavored with shrimp and soy sauce. The wontons are filled with stir-fried garlic shrimp and make explosive mouthfuls of flavor in an otherwise plain soup.

Serves 4

INGREDIENTS

3 cups fish stock
12 fresh shrimp, shelled and with shells and heads removed and set aside
1 tbsp oil
½ tsp freshly chopped parsley
1 small clove garlic, finely chopped
Salt and freshly ground black pepper
12 wonton wrappers
1 egg, beaten
1 tbsp soy sauce

Bring the fish stock to a boil, together with the reserved heads and peelings from the shrimp, then simmer gently for 15 minutes. Pour through a fine strainer, keeping the stock only. Chop 4 of the shrimp. Heat the oil in a wok and stir-fry the chopped shrimp together with the parsley, garlic and salt and pepper to taste. Let cool.

Spread out the wonton wrappers and place a little of the shrimp stuffing on each one. Brush the beaten egg all around the edges of the dough. Fold one side over on to the other, cut the wontons into the desired shape and seal well by pinching the edges together firmly. Set aside to rest for 10 minutes.

Return the stock to a boil, then add the remaining shrimp and the soy sauce. Pinch once more round the edges of the wontons, then carefully place them in the stock. Season with salt and pepper and simmer briskly for 5 minutes. Serve very hot.

CHICKEN & BEANSPROUT SOUP

An ideal soup to make with left-over meat from a cooked chicken, this is quick to prepare and aromatic to the senses.

Serves 4

INGREDIENTS
1½ cups cooked chicken
1½ cups beansprouts
3 cups chicken stock
1 tbsp white wine vinegar
2 tsps sugar
2 tbsps soy sauce
1 tbsp chopped onion
2 shallots, chopped
Salt and freshly ground black
   pepper

Cut the chicken into small dice. Place the beansprouts and stock in a saucepan and bring to a boil. Lower the heat and add the chicken, vinegar, sugar, soy sauce, onion, shallots and salt and pepper to taste. Stir well and simmer the soup for 15 minutes. Serve hot.

BEEF & NOODLE SOUP

*It seems very extravagant to use beef fillet for a soup!
However, with the noodles and seasonings this makes a very
rich and filling soup and is almost a meal in itself.*

Serves 4

INGREDIENTS
½ pound beef fillet or tenderloin
1 large clove garlic, finely
  chopped
1 scallion, chopped
2 tbsps soy sauce
Salt and freshly ground black
  pepper
½ pound fresh egg noodles or
  thin pasta
¼ tsp sesame oil
3 cups beef stock
¼ tsp chili sauce
1 tbsp freshly chopped chives

Cut the beef into thin slices, and
sprinkle with the chopped garlic
and scallion. Sprinkle the soy
sauce over it and season with salt
and pepper. Leave the meat to
marinate for 15 minutes.

Cook the noodles in boiling,
salted water to which the sesame
oil has been added. Rinse them
in cold water and set aside to
drain. Bring the stock to a boil
and add the beef and the
marinade. Simmer gently for 10
minutes. Stir in the noodles,
season with chili sauce and
simmer for just long enough to
heat the noodles through. Serve
with the chives sprinkled over
the top.

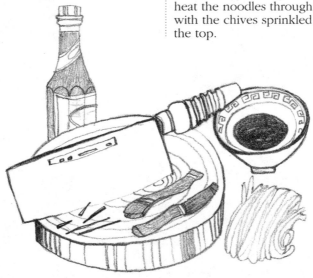

TURKEY SOUP WITH BLACK MUSHROOMS

Frying the turkey in sesame oil gives a delightful fragrance to what can otherwise be a rather bland meat. The mushrooms and ginger combine for extra seasoning in this soup, which may be made economically at any time of year.

Serves 4

INGREDIENTS
⅓ pound turkey breast
1 tbsp sesame oil
1 cup Chinese dried black mushrooms, soaked for 15 minutes in warm water
3 cups chicken stock
1 tbsp soy sauce
1 slice fresh root ginger, peeled and finely chopped
Salt and freshly ground black pepper

Cut the turkey meat into slices and then into small cubes. Heat the sesame oil in a wok and stir-fry the meat until brown. Remove from the pan with a slotted spoon and drain the excess oil from the wok. Cook the mushrooms in boiling, salted water for 10 minutes. Rinse and drain well. Place the mushrooms in a saucepan with the stock. Stir in the turkey, soy sauce, ginger and salt and pepper to taste. Bring to a boil and then simmer gently for 15 minutes. Serve the soup very hot.

RICE SOUP

This is a simple and economical soup to make and is a good way of using up leftover meat; any meat or chicken may be used. The rice makes the soup just a little more substantial.

Serves 4

Ingredients

4 Chinese dried mushrooms, soaked in warm water for 15 minutes
3 cups duck stock
1 scallion, chopped
2 tbsps corn
¼ pound cooked meat, finely diced
Pinch of ground ginger
1 tbsp rice wine
1 tbsp soy sauce
Salt and freshly ground black pepper
1 cup cooked rice

Drain the mushrooms and slice them thinly, discarding the stalks. Place them in a saucepan with the stock and scallion, then add the corn, meat, ginger, rice wine, soy sauce, and salt and pepper to taste. Bring to a boil and simmer for 10 minutes. Stir in the rice and cook for 1 minute. Check the seasoning, adjust as necessary, and serve.

ABALONE SOUP

Abalone is one of those foods, like balsamic vinegar, which has suddenly become very popular in many parts of the world. Abalone are molluscs, about 5 inches in diameter, and it is the muscle that is eaten – so it can be tough. Although popular in Oriental cooking abalone are also found in parts of America. Fresh abalone should be beaten to tenderise them – canned ones do not need this rough treatment!

Serves 4

INGREDIENTS

3 cups fish stock
6 canned abalone plus 2 tbsps
  reserved juice
½ scallion, chopped
1 tbsp soy sauce
2 tsps oyster sauce
1 egg white
Salt and freshly ground black
  pepper

Heat together the fish stock, the reserved abalone juice, scallion, soy sauce and oyster sauce. Cut the canned abalone first into thin slices and then into matchsticks. Add to the stock and simmer gently for 15 minutes. Beat the egg white lightly and then stir it gradually into the boiling soup. Season with salt and pepper to taste and serve.

CHICKEN & SWEETCORN SOUP

I think Chicken & Sweetcorn Soup is probably the most popular Chinese soup in Western restaurants. A little fresh ginger makes it very special.

Serves 4

INGREDIENTS
1½ cups sweetcorn
3 cups chicken stock
2 cooked chicken breasts
12 baby sweetcorns
1-inch piece fresh root ginger, peeled and finely chopped
2 tbsps light soy sauce
Pinch of monosodium glutamate (optional)
¼ tsp chili sauce
Salt and freshly ground black pepper

Place the sweetcorn in a blender or food processor with ½ cup chicken stock and blend until smooth. Pour the purée through a strainer, pushing it through with the back of a spoon.

Cut the cooked chicken into thin slices and place it in a saucepan with the remaining stock. Stir in the sweetcorn purée. Add the baby corn, then bring to a boil. Simmer for 15 minutes. Add the ginger, soy sauce, and monosodium glutamate (if using). Continue cooking for another 10 minutes, then add the chili sauce. Check the seasoning, adding salt and pepper if necessary, and serve.

CRAB SOUP WITH GINGER

This luxurious soup is very special and suitable for even the most lavish entertaining. Shaohsing wine is rice wine; dry sherry could be used instead. If you prefer to use fresh crabmeat, simply combine 10 ounces crabmeat with the well-flavored fish stock, ginger and sake and heat the soup before seasoning to taste.

Serves 4

INGREDIENTS
1 carrot, chopped
1 onion, chopped
½ leek, chopped
1 bay leaf
2 medium-size fresh crabs
3 cups fish stock
1-inch piece of fresh root ginger,
  peeled and chopped
1 tsp Shaohsing wine
Salt and freshly ground black
  pepper

Make a vegetable stock by placing the carrot, onion, leek and bay leaf in a saucepan with a large quantity of water. Bring to a boil and add the crabs. Allow them to boil briskly for 20 minutes or until cooked. Remove the crabs and let them cool. Once cooled, break off the pincers and break the joints, cut open the back and open the claws. Carefully remove all the crabmeat, discarding the gills. Bring the fish stock to a boil and add the ginger, Shaohsing wine and crabmeat. Boil for 15 minutes. Check the seasoning, adding salt and pepper as necessary. Serve very hot.

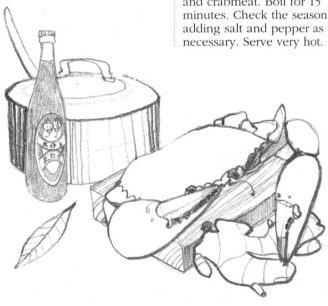

WONTON SOUP

Wonton is to the Chinese what ravioli paste is to the Italians – a means of enclosing a filling for serving in a soup or a sauce. Prepared wonton wrappers are available in specialist food shops.

Serves 6-8

INGREDIENTS
20-24 wonton wrappers
¼ pound finely ground chicken
   or pork
2 tbsps freshly chopped Chinese
   parsley or cilantro leaves
3 scallions, finely chopped
1-inch piece fresh root ginger,
   peeled and grated
1 egg, lightly beaten
6 cups chicken stock
1 tbsp dark soy sauce
¼ tsp sesame oil
Salt and freshly ground black
   pepper
Chinese parsley or watercress for
   garnish

Place all the wonton wrappers on a large, flat surface. Mix together the chicken or pork, chopped Chinese parsley or cilantro, scallions and ginger. Brush the edges of the wrappers lightly with beaten egg. Place a small amount of mixture on one half of each wrapper and fold the other half over the top to form a triangle. Press well to seal the edges.

Bring the stock to a boil in a large saucepan. Add the filled wontons and simmer for 5-10 minutes or until they float to the surface. Add all the remaining ingredients to the soup, using the leaves of the Chinese parsley or watercress for garnish.

CRAB & SWEETCORN SOUP

Crab and sweetcorn make a creamy, fragrant combination of flavors for this soup – you can't beat the flavor of fresh crabmeat.

Serves 4-6

INGREDIENTS
4½ cups fish or chicken stock
1⅓ cups creamed sweetcorn
¼ pound crabmeat
Salt and freshly ground black
   pepper
1 tsp light soy sauce
2 tbsps cornstarch
3 tbsps water or stock
2 egg whites
4 scallions for garnish

Bring the stock to a boil in a large pan. Add the sweetcorn, crabmeat, seasonings and soy sauce, then let simmer for 4-5 minutes. Mix the cornstarch and water or stock and add a spoonful of the hot soup. Add the mixture to the soup and return it to a boil. Cook until the soup thickens. Beat the egg whites until soft peaks form. Stir into the hot soup just before serving. Cut the scallions into thin diagonal slices and scatter over the top to garnish.

APPETIZERS

I could easily start here by saying that these never happen! Well, in the typical way of serving a Chinese meal, any dish that we would consider to be suitable for an appetizer would simply be included in a buffet-style meal! It has really been to satisfy the Western restaurant trade that some classic Chinese dishes have been labeled as appetizers and served as such.

Appetizers, Snacks and Tea Houses

Many Chinese dishes are perfect finger food and make wonderful cocktail nibbles, drinks party snacks and finger food for relaxed and informal entertaining. Such dishes have been enjoyed in China for hundreds of years, but were originally limited to the members of the Imperial Household who had chefs to prepare the snacks for eating throughout the day. They gradually found their way into all Chinese diets and became very popular.

The Chinese would regard these more as tea house dishes. Snacks are served in tea houses all day and there one is more likely to nibble at small quantities of a vast number of foods than have a formal meal. They can be quite time-consuming to prepare and therefore are probably better suited to eating out than preparing at home. Steamed buns, spring rolls and shrimp toasts would all be found on a tea house menu. The variety of foods is much greater than the number of drinks on offer, including teas and wines.

Order "What You Fancy"
"A little of what you fancy does you good" – well, that's a good rule for life but it is often an excuse for over-indulgence! Many Western restaurant menus now include an appetizer called Dim Sum, which literally means eating snacks for pleasure or ordering what you fancy! Whenever I order this I receive a selection of three or four appetizers or snacks, including tiny spring rolls, miniature pork dumplings which are often steamed, and a few small pieces of sparerib – all ideal appetizers!

As dim sum have become more popular, many restaurants specializing in these foods have opened up in the United States, satisfying our Western taste for savory snacks. There is such a variety of dim sum that you can easily make a complete meal out of 10 or 12 varieties.

The recipes that I have selected for this chapter of suggested Chinese appetizers are not the most complicated of the dim sum recipes, but are those which may easily be prepared at home. Some ingredients that we might be tempted to ignore make excellent finger food – chicken wings are virtually impossible to eat decorously with a knife and fork but, coated in honey and soy, they make a delicious Chinese appetizer.

Spring Rolls – the All-time Favorite
Spring Rolls are probably the most popular of all the Chinese appetizers or snacks. They can be served plain, or with a sweet and sour or plum sauce for dipping. The wrappers may be

made at home, but it is easier to buy them ready-made they are sometimes called Chinese Rice Papers. They are dry and brittle and must be brushed with water or held briefly under the cold tap to make them pliable before filling.

Spring Rolls may contain small amounts of shredded chicken or pork, or even a little shellfish, but the main filling ingredients are vegetables, especially beansprouts. These do not require chopping if you are making large rolls to be eaten on a plate, but if you are making smaller rolls to serve as finger food, chop the filling so that it will be possible to bite through the roll without embarrassment!

Spring Rolls are always deep-fried. Drain well on paper towels before serving.

Spareribs in the Oriental Style

Spareribs have always been a popular dish in China but they have also enjoyed enormous success in restaurants around the world. Served outside China the ribs are often very large, but in China they are cut into much smaller pieces, about 2 inches long, and are much more delicate (and easier) to eat.

As Chinese appetizers are predominantly finger food, be sure to offer finger bowls or hot face towels to all those sharing the meal, so that they can clean up, ready for the next course!

CRAB ROLLS

Crab Rolls are prepared in exactly the same way as Spring Rolls. Make certain that the filling is totally enclosed by the wrappers; the outside will become crispy while the filling remains succulently moist.

Serves 4

INGREDIENTS
1 ounce cellophane noodles
⅓ pound crabmeat, fresh or canned
3 scallions, finely sliced
½ tsp grated fresh root ginger
2 tbsps finely chopped bamboo shoots
1 tsp oyster sauce
Salt
12 spring roll wrappers
Vegetable or peanut oil for deep-frying

Soak the cellophane noodles in hot water for 8 minutes, or as directed on the package, then drain. Flake the crabmeat, draining if necessary, then mix it with the scallions, noodles, ginger, bamboo shoots, oyster sauce, and salt to taste. Place the spring roll wrappers on a work surface with a corner pointing towards you. Place a little of the filling just below the center of each. Fold the lower corner over the filling, then fold in the two sides. Roll up, completely enclosing the filling, and damp the edges to seal the rolls – a flour and water paste may be used if necessary. Chill the rolls if they are not to be cooked immediately.

Heat some oil in a wok and deep-fry the crab rolls, four at a time. Drain on paper towels. Serve warm with ginger sauce or sweet and sour sauce.

RICE-COATED MEAT BALLS

*This recipe suggests using ground pork, but chicken, turkey,
beef or lamb could be used with equally good results.*

Serves 4

INGREDIENTS

½ pound ground boned pork
  shoulder
1-inch piece fresh root ginger,
  peeled and chopped
½ tsp finely chopped shallot
½ tsp freshly chopped parsley
½ tsp freshly chopped chives
½ tsp soy sauce
½ egg, beaten
¼ tsp chili sauce
Salt and freshly ground black
  pepper
½ cup long grain rice, pre-
  soaked in warm water for 2
  hours

Mix the meat, ginger, shallots,
parsley, chives, soy sauce, egg
and chili sauce. Beat well to
combine all the ingredients.
Season with salt and pepper and
then form into small meat balls.
Drain the rice very carefully,
shaking well to remove all the
water. Spread the rice over a
work surface. Roll the meat balls
in the rice to coat them evenly.
Steam the meat balls for 15
minutes or until cooked. The
exact cooking time will depend
on the thickness of your
meatballs; small ones take 15
minutes.

RICE PAPER SHRIMP PARCELS

Chinese rice papers are not to be confused with the thick Western variety used as a base for macaroons! They are thin, brittle, almost translucent circles made from a paste of rice flour and water and must be softened with water before being filled.

Serves 4

INGREDIENTS

1⅓ cups medium-size shrimp
1 egg white
½ tsp cornstarch
1 tsp Chinese wine or 2 tsps dry sherry
1 tsp sugar
1 tsp light soy sauce
6 scallions, sliced finely
Salt and freshly ground black pepper
1 package Chinese rice papers
⅔ cup peanut oil

Shell and de-vein the shrimp, and dry on paper towels. Mix the egg white, cornstarch, wine, sugar, soy sauce, scallions and seasoning together, then mix in the shrimp. Heat the peanut oil in a wok until hot. Soften the rice papers by brushing them or dipping them in water – this makes them more manageable. Wrap five or six shrimp in each piece of dampened rice paper. Gently drop the rice paper parcels into hot oil and deep-fry for about 5 minutes. Serve hot.

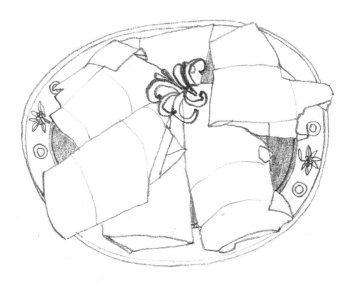

SPRING ROLLS

Spring Rolls make a popular appetizer and are also sometimes served to accompany a main course. Both the wrapper and the enclosed vegetables should be crispy.

Serves 4-6

INGREDIENTS
Wrappers
1 cup all-purpose flour
1 egg, beaten
Cold water

Filling
½ pound pork, trimmed and
  finely shredded
⅔ cup medium-size shrimp
4 scallions, finely chopped
2 tsps chopped fresh root ginger
1 cup shredded Bok Choy
½ cup beansprouts
1 tbsp light soy sauce
A little sesame oil
1 egg, beaten
Oil for deep-frying

For the wrappers, sift the flour into a bowl and make a well in the center. Add the beaten egg and about 1 tbsp cold water. Begin beating with a wooden spoon, gradually drawing in the flour to make a smooth dough. Add more water if necessary. Knead the dough until it is elastic and pliable. Place in a covered bowl and chill for about 4 hours or overnight. Let the dough return to room temperature for 20-30 minutes before rolling out.

Flour a large work surface well and roll the dough out until ¼ inch thick. Cut the dough into 12 squares and then roll each into a larger square about 6 × 6 inches. The dough should be very thin. Cover while preparing the filling.

Cook the pork in 1-2 tbsps oil for about 2-3 minutes. Shell and chop the shrimp. Add it to the pork with the remaining ingredients, except the beaten egg. Cook for a further 2-3 minutes, then let cool.

Lay the wrappers on a clean work surface with the point of each wrapper towards you. Brush the edges lightly with beaten egg. Divide the filling between the 12 wrappers, placing it just above the front point. Fold over the sides like an envelope, then fold over the point until the filling is covered. Roll up like a jelly roll, and press the edges together to seal well.

Heat the oil to 375°F in a deep pan. Depending on the size of the pan, add 2-4 spring rolls at a time and fry until golden brown on both sides. They will float to the surface when one side is brown and should then be turned over. Drain thoroughly on paper towels and serve hot.

SHRIMP TOASTS

*This is one of my favorite Oriental appetizers. I sometimes
serve a chili and cucumber dressing with the toasts, which
are light, savory and delicious.*

Serves 4-6 as an appetizer

INGREDIENTS
1⅓ cups medium-size shrimp
1 small egg, beaten
2 tsps sherry
2 tsps oyster sauce
½ tsp grated fresh root ginger
2 tsps cornstarch
Salt
5 slices white bread
Oil for deep-frying

Shell and de-vein the shrimp.
Chop them finely and combine
in a bowl with the beaten egg,
sherry, oyster sauce, grated
ginger, cornstarch and a pinch of
salt.

Using a 1½-inch round pastry
cutter, cut out circles of bread.
Spread a little of the shrimp
mixture on each, making sure
that all the bread is well covered.
Heat the oil in a wok. Fry the
toasts in batches with the bread
side uppermost, until the bread is
golden brown. Remove the toasts
with a slotted spoon and drain
on paper towels. Keep hot until
all the toasts are cooked.

IMPERIAL PORK ROLLS

These crispy pork rolls are dipped into a spicy sauce before being eaten. This is finger food, so you may like to wrap the Imperial Pork Rolls in lettuce leaves to stop your fingers becoming too greasy.

Serves 4

INGREDIENTS
Dipping Sauce
2 tsps vinegar
1 tbsp water
1 tbsp fish sauce
1 tsp sugar
½ tsp finely chopped fresh root
   ginger
¼ tsp chili sauce

Pork Rolls
4 Chinese dried black
   mushrooms, soaked for 15
   minutes in warm water
¾ pound boneless pork shoulder
½ tsp oil
½ cup beansprouts, blanched
   and drained
1 tbsp soy sauce
½ tsp cornstarch
Salt and freshly ground black
   pepper
Chili sauce
16 sheets Chinese rice paper,
   soaked in warm water for 10
   minutes
1 egg, beaten
½ cup oil

To prepare the sauce, mix together the vinegar, water, fish sauce, sugar and ginger and stand for 30 minutes. Add the chili sauce just before serving.

Dice the mushrooms very finely. Chop the pork very finely and mix with the mushrooms. Heat the oil in a wok and stir-fry the mushrooms and pork with the beansprouts, soy sauce and cornstarch for 2 minutes. Let cool. The mixture should be quite dry. Add salt, pepper and chili sauce to taste.

Drain the rice paper sheets and spread them out on your work surface. Place a little of the cooled stuffing in the center of each sheet, roll it up and seal the edges with a little beaten egg.

Heat the remaining oil in a wok and fry the pork rolls gently on all sides, beginning with the sealed side. Drain on paper towels. Serve the rolls hot, with the dipping sauce in individual bowls.

CROUTON STUDDED "POMEGRANATE" CRISPY SHRIMP BALLS

These shrimp balls make a good appetizer and may also be served as cocktail nibbles or finger food. Cut the croutons very small so that they will stick to the shrimp balls. Serve with stir-fired vegetables as a main course.

Serves 4

INGREDIENTS
4 slices white bread
½ pound flounder fillets
½ pound shrimp, fresh or frozen
2 tsps salt
Freshly ground black pepper to taste
2 egg whites
2 slices fresh root ginger, peeled and finely chopped
2 tbsps cornstarch
Oil for deep-frying

Remove the crusts from the bread, then cut each slice into tiny cubes. Dry in a hot oven until light brown, then spread the croutons out on a large tray. Chop the flounders and shelled shrimps very finely, then mix them with the salt, pepper, egg whites, finely chopped ginger, and cornstarch. Blend well. Shape the mixture into 2-inch balls. Roll over the dried bread croutons to coat the shrimp balls.

Heat the oil in a wok. Add the crouton studded shrimp balls one by one. Turn with a slotted spoon until evenly browned – about 2 minutes. Remove and drain on paper towels. Return to the oil and cook for a further 1 minute. Drain well on paper towels. Serve with good quality soy sauce, catsup and chili sauce as dips.

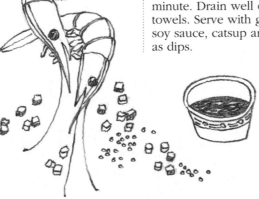

CHINESE OMELET

This is a substantial omelet filled with chicken, ham and shrimp. It will serve four people as an appetizer or two people as a light main course.

Serves 4

INGREDIENTS
2 slices ham
8 cooked shrimp
8 eggs, beaten
1 cup cooked chicken
1 tbsp freshly chopped chives
2 tsps soy sauce
Salt and freshly ground black
    pepper
2 tbsps oil

Chop the ham finely. Shell and chop the shrimp. Mix the eggs, ham, chicken and shrimp together in a bowl. Stir in the chives and soy sauce and check the seasoning, adding salt and pepper to taste. Heat the oil in a skillet and add the omelet mixture. Gently stir the omelet with a fork as it is cooking. Fold over first one side of the omelet and then the other. Serve hot in slices.

HONEY SOY
CHICKEN WINGS

*Do not forget chicken wings – they make the most delicious
finger food. Honey Soy Chicken Wings may be served as part
of a meal or as nibbles with drinks; have plenty of napkins
or warm face cloths ready for sticky fingers.*

Serves 4

INGREDIENTS
2 tbsps peanut oil
1 pound chicken wings
¼ cup light soy sauce
2 tbsps honey
1 tsp sesame seeds
1 clove garlic, crushed
1 tsp grated fresh root ginger
½ tsp salt

Heat a wok, add the oil and, when hot, add the chicken wings. Fry for 10 minutes. Carefully strain off any excess oil. Add the soy sauce, honey, sesame seeds, garlic, grated ginger and salt to the chicken in the wok. Lower the heat. Simmer for 20 minutes, turning the chicken wings occasionally. Serve hot or cold.

SESAME CHICKEN WINGS

Any recipe using chicken wings is economical to prepare as they are relatively cheap to buy. It is hopeless to attempt to eat these with a knife and fork; this is real finger food!

Serves 8

INGREDIENTS
12 chicken wings
1 tbsp salted black beans
1 tbsp water
1 tbsp oil
2 cloves garlic, crushed
2 slices fresh root ginger, peeled
 and cut into fine shreds
3 tbsps soy sauce
1½ tbsps dry sherry or rice wine
Large pinch of freshly ground
 black pepper
1 tbsp sesame seeds
Scallions or Chinese parsley to
 garnish (optional)

Using a sharp, heavy knife, cut off and discard the wing tips, then cut through the joint and separate the wing into two pieces. Crush the beans and add the water. Leave to stand for a few minutes.

Heat the oil in a wok and add the garlic and ginger. Stir briefly and add the chicken wings. Cook for about 3 minutes, stirring, until the chicken is lightly browned. Add the soy sauce and wine and stir-fry for a further 30 seconds. Add the soaked black beans and pepper.

Cover the wok tightly and simmer for about 8-10 minutes. Uncover and turn up the heat. Continue stirring until the liquid has almost evaporated and the chicken wings are glazed with the sauce. Remove from the heat and sprinkle with the sesame seeds, stirring to coat the wings completely. Serve, garnished with scallions or Chinese parsley, if wished.

QUICK FRY
"CRYSTAL SHRIMP"

This recipe is very quick to prepare, light in flavor and not too spicy. Sprinkling the vinegar over the shrimp at the last moment really helps to bring out their flavor.

Serves 4

INGREDIENTS
1 pound fresh shrimp
1 egg white
1 tbsp cornstarch
⅓ cup oil
1 tsp finely chopped fresh root ginger
2 tsps chopped onion
½ tsp salt
1 tbsp pale dry sherry
2 tbsps fish, vegetable or chicken stock
2 tsps vinegar

Clean, shell and de-vein the shrimp. Mix together the egg white and cornstarch, add the shrimp and coat well. Heat the oil in a wok, add the shrimp and stir-fry over low heat for 2-3 minutes until the color changes. Remove the shrimp with a slotted spoon. Pour off any excess oil from the wok. Add the chopped ginger, onion, salt, sherry and stock and bring to a boil. Return the shrimp to the wok and stir over the heat for a few seconds until hot. Sprinkle with vinegar and serve.

63

BARBECUED SPARERIBS

This is real finger-food – there is no delicate way of eating spareribs! Have plenty of finger bowls or warm face cloths ready for sticky fingers.

Serves 4-6

INGREDIENTS
4-6 scallions for garnish
4 pounds pork spareribs
3 tbsps dark soy sauce
⅓ cup hoisin sauce (Chinese barbecue sauce)
2 tbsps dry sherry
¼ tsp five-spice powder
1 tbsp brown sugar

First prepare the garnish. Trim the roots and the dark green tops from the scallions. Cut both ends into thin strips, leaving about ½ inch in the middle uncut. Place the scallions in ice water for several hours or overnight so that the ends curl up.

Cut the spareribs into single ribs, if the butcher has not already done so. Mix all the remaining ingredients together, pour over the ribs and stir to coat evenly. Leave to marinate for 1 hour.

Place the sparerib pieces on a rack in a roasting pan containing 2½ cups water, then cook in a 350°F oven for 30 minutes. Add more hot water to the pan if necessary while cooking.

Turn the ribs over and brush with the remaining sauce. Cook for a further 30 minutes or until tender. Serve garnished with the scallions.

CARAMELIZED SPARERIBS

The honey in the sauce will caramelize on the spareribs, giving them a sweet flavor and a lovely sticky glaze. Do keep an eye on the ribs during cooking and turn them if they start to brown too much.

Serves 4

INGREDIENTS
1 carrot
1 leek
1 bay leaf
2 pounds pork spareribs, separated
1 tbsp honey
1 tbsp white wine vinegar
1 tsp chopped garlic
2 tbsps soy sauce
¼ cup chicken stock
Salt and freshly ground black pepper

Put plenty of water in a large saucepan with the carrot, leek and bay leaf. Bring to a boil and add the spareribs. Blanch the meat for 10 minutes, then remove the ribs from the pan and drain well. Put the ribs side by side in a baking dish. Combine the honey, vinegar and garlic, and spread the mixture on the ribs. Add the soy sauce and chicken stock to the dish. Season well with salt and pepper.

Cook in a 475°F oven for 20 minutes, or until the ribs have caramelized and turned a rich, dark brown color.

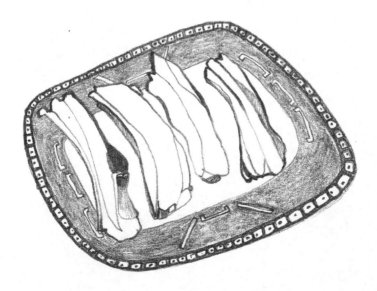

FRIED CHINESE RAVIOLI WITH SALMON

Wontons are very similar to Italian ravioli – little parcels of dough which may be filled with countless stuffings. These contain fresh salmon and chives – delicious! As they are fried they require no sauce – boiled ravioli always needs sauce.

Serves 4

INGREDIENTS
¾ pound fresh salmon
.1 tbsp freshly chopped chives
A little lemon juice
Salt and freshly ground black
  pepper
24 wonton wrappers
1 egg, beaten
Oil for deep-frying

Prepare the salmon by boning, filleting and finely chopping it.

Mix the salmon with the chives, lemon juice, salt and pepper. Lay out 12 wonton wrappers and divide the stuffing evenly between them, placing it in the center of each wrapper. Brush the beaten egg around the edges of the stuffing and top with the remaining 12 wrappers. Cut each ravioli into the shape you choose and seal the edges firmly by pinching with your fingers or pushing down with a fork. Set aside to rest for 15 minutes.

Heat the oil to 340˚F. Cook a few wonton ravioli at a time in the hot oil. Remove when cooked and drain on paper towels. Season with salt and pepper and serve immediately.

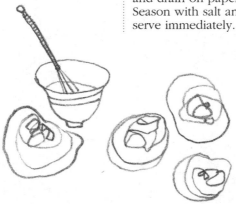

CRISPY WONTON SAUCE

*Wonton skins are available in Chinese supermarkets. They
are usually filled with spiced ground pork or dried baby
shrimp, but you can experiment with your own fillings.
Deep-fry the wontons until crispy.*

*The wontons should be dipped in a sauce for eating. The
same sauce may be used for dipping any finger foods.*

INGREDIENTS
1 tbsp cornstarch
1 tbsp tomato paste
1 tbsp vinegar
1 tbsp soy sauce
2 tbsps sugar
1½ tbsps oil

Place all the sauce ingredients in
a pan and stir together over
medium heat for 4-5 minutes.

FISH & SHELLFISH

Fish and shellfish play an important role in Chinese cooking and I have heard that there are at least two hundred varieties of fish in common use! The recipes in this chapter concentrate on the few most popular varieties in use throughout the country.

Fish from River and Sea
China's coastline provides wonderful fish and especially shellfish, although the marine fishing industry is relatively undeveloped. Lobster, crab, scallops and mussels are all freely available, although sea fish only accounts for about one-quarter

of the total catch each year. In refreshing contrast to the coastal waters of so many other countries, the Chinese fishing grounds are relatively under-fished.

The majority of fish eaten in China comes either from the rivers or from fish farms. The latter are not a new concept – carp have been farmed for many years in special pools and this technique is now being used for a variety of species. The fish farms are often close to major cities as it is considered of utmost importance that no more than three or four hours should pass between the killing and the eating of the fish. It is quite common for live fish to be sold in markets in China.

China has two major rivers, the Yangtze and the Hwang Ho or Yellow River, and numerous smaller waterways, lakes and canals. They all provide numerous varieties of fish, and porgy, bass and trout are widely available and very popular.

Fish as Meat!

The main advantage of fish is that it is even quicker to cook than meat! Many Chinese dishes treat it in quite a robust way, serving it in a well-flavored sauce which might mask a delicate flavor. I like to cook strong, gamy fish such as red mullet in this way and to attempt to preserve the more delicate flavors of other fish in milder dishes.

Fish requires only light cooking. For example, although shrimp or other fish may be served deep-fried with a sweet and sour or chili sauce, the sauce will be poured over the fish balls just before serving. Fried meat cooked in the same way is usually simmered in the sauce for a short time before serving.

Brush up your Filleting Skills

The Chinese are very fond of preparing and cooking whole fish, often by steaming. Shreds of fresh root ginger and scallions are scattered over the fish for flavoring and a spicy sauce, prepared in a separate pan during the steaming, will be served to accompany the fish. Steamed Fish in Ginger is an example of a whole fish which is stuffed, then steamed. You will need a heatproof plate that will fit inside a steamer to cook in this way. It is a good idea to brush up on your fish filleting skills in order to remove the fillets neatly from the bones for serving, although large pieces of fish served on a bed of stir-fried vegetables or noodles do look very attractive. I love serving trout in this way.

Fresh is Best

The Chinese always pay particular attention to the freshness of their fish and this also applies to shellfish. They would always use uncooked shrimp and shellfish, cooking even their own crabs and lobsters just before use. Many Westerners would not do this and therefore the use of prepared or canned crabmeat has crept into recipes adapted for the Western kitchen. It is sometimes possible to buy uncooked shrimp in fresh fish shops and supermarkets and these have a much more piquant flavor than those which have been cooked and frozen. Do try them – they are a little more expensive than cooked shrimp but the flavor is well worth the expense.

Abalone – the New Fish of the Orient

Abalone have recently become popular in the West, where they are wrongly regarded as an Eastern delicacy. Yes, they are widely used in Chinese cooking, but there are smaller varieties of abalone freely available on the west coast of the United States.

Abalone are a variety of shellfish, a mollusc similar to a mussel. The part which is eaten is the muscle which holds the shell closed and consequently it tends to be rather tough and chewy. Abalone may be bought fresh or canned. I think that the canning process does slightly soften or tenderize the fish – perhaps abalone are the exception to the rule that fresh is best?

DEEP-FRIED SEA BASS

In this recipe the bass is partly cooked by frying and then finished in a tangy, spicy sauce. Rinse the pickled cabbage under running water before adding it to the dish.

Serves 4

INGREDIENTS
1½ pounds sea bass
3 tsps dark soy sauce
2 tbsps cornstarch
3¾ cups oil
2 ounces ground pork
2 cloves garlic
2 small chilies
2 scallions
1 slice fresh root ginger, peeled
2½ cups chicken stock
2 tsps salt
¾ cup pickled cabbage
2 tsps sesame oil

Clean the fish. Make diagonal cuts across the surface and rub the soy sauce over the fish. Mix the cornstarch to a smooth paste with 2 tbsps water.

Heat the oil in a wok to about 375°F, then carefully add the fish. Brown the fish on both sides, then remove with a slotted spoon and drain on paper towels.

Remove all but ¼ cup of the oil then reheat the wok. Add the pork, chopped garlic, chilis, scallions, ginger, stock, salt and pickled cabbage. Stir-fry for 1-2 minutes. Return the fish to the wok and cook for a further 10 minutes. Remove the fish and put on a heated serving plate. Pour the cornstarch mixture into the wok and cook for 1-2 minutes, until boiling and thickened. Add the sesame oil, then pour the mixture over the fish and serve.

SINGAPORE FISH

Curries from Singapore and Malaysia often include fruit.
The Chinese influence on the cuisine of Singapore is obvious
— and from Singapore the Chinese learned about
curry spices.

Serves 6

INGREDIENTS

1 pound flounder fillets
1 egg white
1 tbsp cornstarch
2 tsps white wine
Salt and freshly ground black
  pepper
Oil for frying
1 large onion, cut into ½-inch
  thick wedges
1 tbsp mild curry powder
8-ounce can pineapple pieces,
  drained and juice reserved, or
  ½ fresh pineapple, peeled and
  cubed
11-ounce can mandarin orange
  segments, drained and juice
  reserved
1 tbsp cornstarch
Juice of 1 lime
2 tsps sugar (optional)
8-ounce can sliced water
  chestnuts, drained

Skin the flounder fillets using a
sharp knife. Start at the tail end
of each fillet. Slide the knife back
and forward along the length of
each, cutting the fish flesh away
from the skin. Cut the fish into
even-size pieces – about 2
inches.

Mix together the egg white,
cornstarch, wine, salt and
pepper. Place the fish in the
mixture and leave to stand while
heating the oil in a large pan or
wok. When the oil is hot, fry a
few pieces of fish at a time until
light golden brown and crispy.
Remove the fish using a slotted
spoon and drain on paper
towels. Continue frying until all
the fish is cooked.

Remove all except 1 tbsp of the
oil from the wok and add the
onion. Stir-fry for 1-2 minutes
and then add the curry powder.
Cook for a further 1-2 minutes.
Add the juices from the
pineapple and mandarin oranges
and bring to a boil.

Combine the cornstarch and lime
juice into a paste and add a
spoonful of the boiling fruit juice.
Add the mixture to the wok and
cook for about 2 minutes until
thickened. Taste and add sugar if
necessary. Add the fruit, water
chestnuts and fried fish to the
wok and stir until coated. Heat
through for 1 minute and serve
immediately.

STEAMED FISH WITH BLACK BEANS

Black beans can be stored in an air-tight container in the refrigerator for several weeks after opening, and may also be frozen. To test the fish to see if it is cooked, pull back the skin and insert the tip of a sharp knife – the fish is cooked if the knife goes in easily.

Serves 4

INGREDIENTS

2 pounds whole snapper, bass or porgy, cleaned and scaled
2 cloves garlic, crushed
1 tbsp salted black beans
½ tsp cornstarch
1 tsp sesame oil
1 tbsp light soy sauce
1 tsp sugar
1 tsp Chinese wine *or* 2 tsps dry sherry
Salt and freshly ground black pepper
4-ounce can bamboo shoots, cut into shreds

Wash and clean the fish and dry with paper towels. Make 3 or 4 diagonal cuts in the flesh of the fish on each side. Rub garlic into the cuts and place the fish on a flat baking dish. Rinse the black beans in cold water, then crush them with the back of a spoon. Add the cornstarch, sesame oil, soy sauce, sugar, wine or sherry, salt and pepper and mix well. Pour the sauce over the fish, then sprinkle the bamboo shoots on top. Put the dish in the top of a bamboo steamer or on a metal trivet standing in a wok. Add water, ensuring the level is below the dish. Cover and bring to a boil. Steam for about 10 minutes. Make sure that the fish is cooked, but do not oversteam. Serve hot.

SWEET-SOUR FISH

This is an easy but impressive way of cooking a whole fish for two people – I would serve it with stir-fried vegetables. In China a river or freshwater fish would be used but a small sea bass is just as good.

Serves 2

INGREDIENTS

1 sea bass, gray mullet or carp, weighing about 2 pounds, cleaned and scaled
1 tbsp dry sherry
2-3 slices fresh root ginger, peeled
½ cup sugar
⅓ cup cider vinegar
1 tbsp soy sauce
2 tbsps cornstarch
1 clove garlic, crushed
2 scallions, shredded
1 small carrot, peeled and finely shredded
2 tbsps shredded bamboo shoots

Rinse the fish well inside and out. Make three diagonal cuts on each side of the fish with a sharp knife. Trim off the fins, leaving the dorsal fin on top, and trim the tail to two neat points.

Bring enough water to a boil in a wok to cover the fish. Gently lower the fish into the boiling water and add the sherry and ginger. Cover the wok tightly and remove it at once from the heat. Leave to stand 15-20 minutes to let the fish cook in the residual heat. To test if the fish is cooked, pull the dorsal fin – if it comes off easily the fish is done. If not, return the wok to the heat and bring to a boil. Remove from the heat and leave the fish to stand a further 5 minutes. Transfer the fish to a heated serving dish and keep it warm.

Remove all but ¼ cup of the cooking liquid from the wok. Add the remaining ingredients including the vegetables and cook, stirring constantly, until the sauce thickens. Spoon some of the sauce over the fish and serve the rest separately.

CRISPY FISH WITH CHILI

A technique of double frying is used in this recipe to get the batter coating on the fish really crispy. The sweet, hot chili sauce makes a perfect match for the fish.

Serves 4

INGREDIENTS
Oil for deep-frying
1 pound flounder fillets, skinned, boned, and cut into 1-inch cubes

Batter
½ cup all-purpose flour
Salt
1 egg, separated
1 tbsp oil
⅓ cup milk

Sauce
1 tsp grated fresh root ginger
¼ tsp chili powder
2 tbsps tomato paste
2 tbsps tomato relish
2 tbsps dark soy sauce
2 tbsps Chinese wine or dry sherry
2 tbsps water
1 tsp sugar
1 red chili, de-seeded and finely sliced
1 clove garlic, crushed
Salt and freshly ground black pepper

Prepare the batter. Sift the flour with a pinch of salt into a bowl. Make a well in the center, and drop in the egg yolk and oil. Mix to a smooth batter with the milk, gradually incorporating the flour. Beat well, then cover and set aside in a cool place for 30 minutes. Beat the egg white until stiff, and stir into the batter just before using.

Heat the oil for deep-frying in a wok. Dip the fish pieces into the batter to coat them completely. When the oil is hot, carefully lower in the fish pieces and fry for about 10 minutes until cooked through and golden brown. Remove the fish with a slotted spoon. Reheat the oil and re-fry each fish piece for a further 2 minutes. Remove with a slotted spoon and drain on paper towels.

Carefully remove all but 1 tbsp of oil from the wok. Reheat the oil, and add all the sauce ingredients with salt and pepper to taste. Stir well over moderate heat for 3 minutes. Turn up the heat and add the fish pieces. Coat with the sauce and, when heated through, serve immediately.

STEAMED FISH IN GINGER

Steaming is an excellent method of cooking fish, keeping it moist and preserving all the delicate flavors. Smaller fish, such as red mullet, may be cooked in this way but I think that a whole large fish looks much more impressive.

Serves 4

INGREDIENTS

3 pounds whole snapper, bass or porgy, cleaned and scaled
6 scallions, cut into 2-inch lengths, then into fine shreds
3 pieces fresh root ginger, peeled and cut into fine shreds
Lemon slices and parsley to garnish (optional)

Stuffing

1 cup cooked rice
1 tsp grated fresh root ginger
3 scallions, finely sliced
2 tsps light soy sauce

Prepare the stuffing. Mix together the cooked rice, grated ginger, scallions and soy sauce. Stuff the rice mixture into the cleaned fish cavity, packing it in well. Place the stuffed fish on a flat baking dish, and arrange strips of scallion and ginger on top. Put the dish on top of a bamboo steamer or metal trivet standing in a wok. Add water, ensuring the water level is below the dish. Cover and bring to a boil. Steam for 10 minutes. Make sure that the fish is just cooked – be sure not to oversteam and toughen it. Serve hot, garnished with lemon slices and parsley if wished.

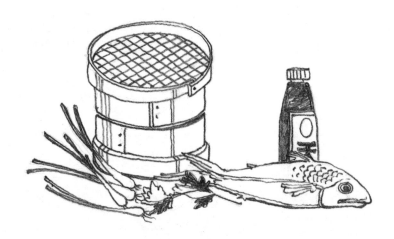

SZECHUAN FISH

To serve Szechuan fish garnished with chili flowers you will need to prepare the chilies at least four hours in advance of cooking the dish. Choose the long, thin chilies – a mixture of red and green will look very effective.

Serves 6

INGREDIENTS
6 red and green chilies for
   garnish
1 pound flounder fillets
Salt and freshly ground black
   pepper
1 egg
⅔ cup flour
⅓ cup white wine
Oil for frying
⅓ cup diced cooked ham
1-inch piece fresh ginger, finely
   diced
½-1 red or green chili, peeled
   and de-seeded, finely diced
6 water chestnuts, finely diced
4 scallions, finely chopped
3 tbsps light soy sauce
1 tsp cider vinegar or rice wine
   vinegar
½ tsp ground Szechuan pepper
   (optional)
1¼ cups fish or vegetable stock
1 tbsp cornstarch mixed with 2
   tbsps water
2 tsps sugar

For the garnish, choose unblemished chilies with stems on. Using a small, sharp knife, cut the chilies into strips. Starting from the pointed end, cut down to within ½ inch of the stem end. Rinse out the seeds under cold running water and place the chilies in ice water. Leave to soak for at least 4 hours or overnight until they open up.

Cut the flounder fillets into 2-inch pieces and season with salt and pepper. Beat the egg well and add the flour and wine to make a batter. Dredge the fish lightly with extra flour and then dip it into the batter. Coat the fish well. Heat a wok and, when hot, add enough oil to deep-fry the fish. When the oil is hot, fry a few pieces of fish at a time, until golden brown. Drain the fish pieces on paper towels and repeat until all the fish is cooked.

Remove all but 1 tbsp of oil from the wok and add the ham, ginger, diced chili, water chestnuts and scallions. Cook for about 1 minute, then add the soy sauce and vinegar. If using Szechuan pepper, add it now. Stir well and cook for 1 further minute. Remove the vegetables from the pan and set them aside. Pour the stock into the wok and bring to a boil. When boiling, add 1 spoonful of the hot stock to the cornstarch mixture. Add the mixture to the stock and reboil, stirring constantly until thickened. Stir in the sugar and return the fish and vegetables to the sauce. Heat through for 30 seconds and serve immediately.

BAKED TROUT WITH BLACK BEAN SAUCE

This is a very robust way of cooking trout – and it is very delicious! Any whole fish could be cooked in this way. Prepare the various mixtures before you start the fish.

Serves 4

INGREDIENTS

1½ pounds trout (cleaned, with head on)
1 tsp salt
½ tsp pepper
½ tsp ground ginger
2 tbsps shredded scallions
1 tbsp shredded fresh root ginger
2 tbsps vegetable oil
1 tbsp black bean sauce
1 tsp chopped dried red chili
½ tsp sugar
1 tbsp light soy sauce
1 tbsp pale dry sherry
1 tbsp shredded scallion
½ tbsp shredded fresh root ginger
¼ tbsp shredded red chili
1 tbsp light soy sauce
1 tsp sesame oil

Lightly score the fish by making diagonal cuts at 1-inch intervals on both sides of the body. Mix together the salt, pepper and ground ginger. Rub this mixture over the inside and outside of the fish. Lay the fish in a baking dish. Scatter the shredded scallions and root ginger over the fish. Heat the vegetable oil in a small pan until almost smoking and pour over the fish. Mix together the black bean sauce, dried chili, sugar, light soy sauce and sherry. Spoon the mixture over the fish and cover the dish tightly with foil. Cook for 15-20 minutes in a 400°F oven.

Mix together the 1 tbsp shredded scallion, ½ tbsp shredded root ginger and ¼ tbsp shredded red chili. When the fish is cooked, pile the shredded vegetables on top of the fish and trickle with the soy sauce and sesame oil before serving.

TROUT FILLETS WITH GINGER & SCALLION

Sea trout are larger than river trout; use either fish for this recipe. The sauce is slightly sweet and finishes the dish perfectly.

Serves 4

INGREDIENTS
4 sea trout fillets
Salt and freshly ground black
    pepper
1 scallion, chopped
1 tsp chopped fresh root ginger
½ cup white wine vinegar
½ cup soy sauce
3 tsps sugar
½ cup fish stock

Season the trout fillets with salt and pepper. Lay them in a steamer basket and scatter the scallion and ginger over. Set to one side. Mix the vinegar, soy sauce, sugar and fish stock together in a saucepan. Heat until boiling and let reduce and thicken. Steam the trout for about 5 minutes while the sauce is cooking, then serve the fillets with the sauce spooned over.

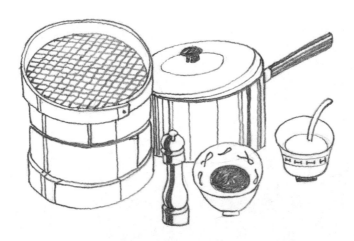

PORGY WITH PINEAPPLE

Pineapple is widely used in Oriental cooking – it has a sweet freshness which helps to bring out the flavor of other ingredients, and it complements fish particularly well.

Serves 4

INGREDIENTS
1 large porgy
2 tbsps oil
1-2 cloves garlic, finely chopped
4 slices of canned pineapple, cut into small pieces
1 tbsp soy sauce
¼ cup pineapple syrup, from the can
1¼ cups fish stock
1 tsp cornstarch, combined with a little water
Salt and freshly ground black pepper

Cut the fins off the fish, and remove the fillets with a sharp knife. Skin the fillets and cut into bite-size pieces. Discard the head, tail and bones or save them for stock.

Heat 1 tbsp of the oil in a wok and stir-fry the garlic and the pineapple pieces. Pour off any excess oil and add the soy sauce, pineapple syrup and fish stock. Let the sauce reduce a little and then add the cornstarch paste, stirring continuously until the sauce boils and thickens. Remove the sauce from the wok and keep warm. Heat the remaining oil in the cleaned wok and stir-fry the pieces of fish, seasoning them with salt and pepper. Shake the wok frequently to cook the fish evenly. Serve the porgy with the sauce spooned over the fish.

WHITING FRITTERS WITH COLD FISH SAUCE

Whiting is a very under-rated fish. It is relatively cheap to buy and has a good flavor and texture. You will need to fry the fish in several batches to prevent the pieces from sticking together, so put the cooked whiting in a warm oven until cooking is complete.

Serves 4

INGREDIENTS
1½ cups sifted all-purpose flour
1 tsp baking powder
½ cup water
1 egg, beaten
1 tsp oil
1 pound whiting fillets
Salt and freshly ground black
  pepper
Oil for deep-frying

Sauce
1 tbsp fish sauce
1 tbsp soy sauce
1 tbsp fish stock
1 tsp freshly chopped mint

Make a batter by mixing the sifted flour and the baking powder together in a bowl, then mixing in the water, followed by the egg. Add the oil and a large pinch of salt and beat all the ingredients together well. Set the batter aside to rest for a few minutes.

Season the whiting fillets with salt and pepper and cut them into thin strips. Heat the oil for deep-frying. Dip the whiting strips into the batter and fry them in the hot oil until crispy and golden. Remove the fritters with a slotted spoon and drain them on paper towels. Keep hot.

Meanwhile, mix together the sauce ingredients and serve the sauce with the hot whiting fritters.

GOOSEFISH WITH ONIONS & VINEGAR SAUCE

Goosefish is a firm-fleshed white fish which keeps its shape well during cooking. The onion and vinegar sauce is slightly sharp and very Oriental.

Serves 4

INGREDIENTS
2 pounds goosefish tail, cleaned
2 tbsps oil
2 large onions, finely sliced
2 tbsps white wine vinegar
2 tsps sugar
1 tbsp soy sauce
1½ cups fish stock
½ tsp chopped fresh root ginger
Salt and freshly ground black
   pepper
1 tbsp cornstarch

Prepare the fish by pulling off the skin. Fillet the fish by sliding a sharp knife between the flesh and the central bones on each side. Cut both fillets in half.

Heat the oil in a wok. Add the onions and stir-fry gently until soft, then ease them up the sides of the wok. Add the fish fillets to the wok, stir-fry for 1 minute, then push the onions back into the wok with the fish. Add the vinegar to the pan and boil until almost evaporated, then stir in the sugar, soy sauce, fish stock and ginger. Season with salt and pepper to taste. Stir well, cover and cook gently for 7-8 minutes. Remove the fish from the wok, cut into thin slices and keep warm on a hot plate or in a warm oven. Mix the cornstarch to a paste with a little cold water, add to the sauce and stir continuously until boiling and thickened. Place the onions and their sauce on a hot serving plate. Place the sliced fish on top and serve immediately.

SEA BASS IN FIVE-SPICE SAUCE

This delicious sauce is wonderful with fish and is also
excellent with pork, which may then be barbecued – I use it
to marinate pork tenderloin.

Serves 4

INGREDIENTS
1 pound sea bass fillets
1 tbsp fish sauce
1 tbsp Chinese wine
1 tsp oyster sauce
½ tsp finely chopped fresh root
    ginger
2 shallots, chopped
2 tsps five-spice powder
Salt and freshly ground black
    pepper
1 tbsp oil

Cut the sea bass fillets into thin slices and arrange the slices on a plate. Combine the fish sauce, wine, oyster sauce, chopped ginger, shallots and five-spice powder and pour over the fish. Season the fish with salt and pepper and leave to marinate in the sauce mixture for 1 hour.

Heat the oil in a skillet. Drain the fish slices and fry briefly for 30 seconds on each side. Serve immediately. The sauce may be heated and served with the fish.

PORGY IN SWEET &
SOUR SAUCE

Porgy is a lovely fish with a delicious flavor. Don't be afraid that the sweet and sour sauce will mask the flavor of the fish – they complement each other well.

Serves 4

INGREDIENTS

1 porgy, weighing about 1¾ pounds
½ red pepper, de-seeded
½ green pepper, de-seeded
¼ cucumber
1 tbsp oil
1 tsp finely chopped fresh root ginger
2 cloves garlic, finely chopped
2 scallions, finely chopped
¼ small fresh green chili, de-seeded
3 tbsps pineapple juice
2 tbsps crushed tomato or tomato sauce
⅔ cup fish stock
1 tsp cornstarch, combined with a little water
1 tbsp vinegar
Salt and freshly ground black pepper
1 sheet dried seaweed (optional)
1 tbsp freshly chopped chives to garnish

Scale and clean the porgy then fillet the fish, removing any bones, and cut into medium-size pieces. Cut the red and green peppers and the cucumber into fine strips.

Heat the oil in a wok and cook the vegetables, ginger, garlic, scallion and the chili for 1 minute. Add the pineapple juice, the crushed tomato or tomato sauce and the fish stock. Simmer over low heat for 2 minutes. Thicken the sauce with the cornstarch paste, stirring continuously until boiling. Remove and discard the chili, add the vinegar and season with salt and pepper to taste.

Steam the porgy over water containing strips of the dried seaweed, if using. Serve the fish accompanied by the sweet and sour sauce and sprinkled with the chopped chives.

CHINESE RAW FISH

Don't decide that raw fish is not to your taste before you have tried it! The secret is to slice the fish very thinly and to allow at least 30 minutes for it to marinate.

Serves 4

INGREDIENTS
½ pound firm-fleshed fish fillets, e.g. haddock or cod
½ pound sea bass
1 tsp finely chopped fresh root ginger
1-2 cloves garlic, finely chopped
1 tsp finely chopped shallot
Juice of 1 lemon
10 coriander seeds, crushed
¼ tsp sesame oil
Salt and freshly ground black pepper
1 tbsp freshly chopped chives to garnish

Slice the fish very thinly. Spread the slices out on a plate and sprinkle with the chopped ginger, garlic and shallot. Trickle with the lemon juice and sprinkle with the crushed coriander seeds, then finally add the sesame oil. Allow to marinate for 30 minutes. Season with salt and pepper to taste, garnish with the chopped chives and serve.

TROUT IN OYSTER SAUCE

This is a most unusual way to serve trout but it is delicious!
The orange juice is a wonderful flavoring.

Serves 4

INGREDIENTS
2 trout
Salt and freshly ground black
  pepper
2 tbsps oyster sauce
½ cup bamboo shoots, cut into
  matchsticks
1 tbsp oil
1 tsp finely chopped fresh root
  ginger
1-2 cloves garlic, finely chopped
½ green pepper, de-seeded and
  finely chopped
½ red pepper, de-seeded and
  finely chopped
½ onion, finely chopped
1 tsp sugar
1 tsp white wine vinegar
Juice of ½ orange
2 tbsps soy sauce
1 cup fish stock
1 tsp cornstarch, combined with
  a little water

Fillet the trout, then cut each fillet into several pieces. Season with salt and pepper, and brush each one with oyster sauce. Stack in pairs and set aside. Blanch the bamboo shoots, then rinse and let them drain.

Heat the oil in a wok and stir-fry the ginger, garlic, peppers, onion and bamboo shoots for 2-3 minutes. Add the sugar, vinegar, orange juice, soy sauce and fish stock and cook for 3 minutes. Season to taste, then add the cornstarch, stirring continuously until boiling and thickened. Steam the trout pieces separately for approximately 3 minutes, or until just cooked. Serve the fish on a bed of the vegetables in sauce.

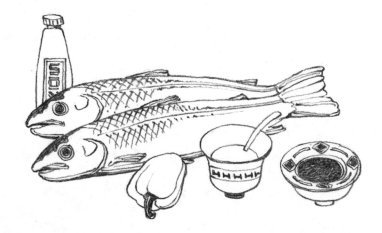

STEAMED SEA BASS

Shred the root ginger and scallion garnish for this steamed bass very finely for maximum flavor. If the fish is too large to lay across a flat dish in your steamer, curl it round on its belly.

Serves 4

INGREDIENTS
1 whole sea bass weighing about
    1½ pounds
2 scallions
1-2 strips bacon
2 slices fresh root ginger, peeled
    and chopped

Sauce and Garnish
3-4 slices fresh root ginger
2 scallions
1½ tbsps soy sauce
1 tbsp pale dry sherry
1½ tbsps oil

Clean the fish. Chop the scallions into 2-inch pieces and chop the bacon finely.

Prepare the sauce and garnish. Cut the 3-4 slices ginger and the scallions into fine shreds. Mix together the soy sauce and sherry. Place the bass on a baking dish that will fit in your steamer and scatter the chopped scallions, the chopped ginger and the bacon over the fish. Place the dish in the steamer, cover and steam well for 15-20 minutes. Remove the chopped vegetables and bacon from the fish.

Pour the sherry and soy mixture over the fish just before serving and garnish with the shredded ginger and scallions. Heat the oil until almost smoking and pour over the fish, creating a loud sizzle. Serve immediately.

KUNG PAO SHRIMP WITH CASHEW NUTS

*I love cashew nuts with shrimp, with chicken, on their own –
any way! Perhaps Kung Pao felt the same way, but no-one
seems to know who the creator of this recipe actually was!*

Serves 6

INGREDIENTS
½ tsp chopped fresh root ginger
1 tsp chopped garlic
1½ tbsps cornstarch
¼ tsp baking soda
Salt and freshly ground black
  pepper
¼ tsp sugar
1 pound uncooked shrimp
¼ cup oil
1 small onion, chopped
1 large or 2 small zucchini, cut
  into ½-inch cubes
1 small red pepper, cut into
  ½-inch cubes
⅓ cup cashew nuts

Sauce
¾ cup chicken stock
1 tbsp cornstarch
2 tsps chili sauce
2 tsps bean paste (optional)
2 tsps sesame oil
1 tbsp dry sherry or rice wine

Mix together the ginger, garlic,
cornstarch, baking soda, salt,
pepper and sugar. If the shrimp
are not shelled, remove the shells
and the dark vein running along
the rounded side. Cut any large
shrimp into 2. Add the shrimp to
the dry ingredients and leave to
stand for 20 minutes.

Heat the oil in a wok and, when
hot, add the shrimp and
flavorings. Cook, stirring over
high heat, for about 20 seconds,
or until the shrimp change color.
Transfer to a plate using a slotted
spoon. Add the onion to the
same oil in the wok and cook for
about 1 minute, then add the
zucchini and red pepper and
cook for about 30 seconds. Mix
the sauce ingredients together
and add them to the wok. Cook,
stirring constantly, until the sauce
is slightly thickened. Return the
shrimp to the wok with the
cashew nuts and cook until
heated through completely.

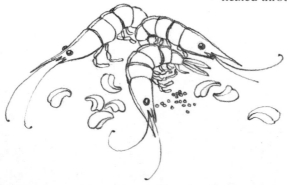

CRAB WITH BAMBOO SHOOTS

Depending on where you live, you may be able to get fresh crabs in season. Canned crabmeat is a good alternative.

Serves 4

INGREDIENTS
1 green or red chili
¾ pound crabmeat
1 cup bamboo shoots
1 tbsp oil
4 slices fresh root ginger, peeled
½ onion, chopped
1 tsp vinegar
1 tsp sugar
1 cup fish stock
1 tsp cornstarch, blended with a little water
Salt and freshly ground black pepper
1 tbsp freshly chopped chives

Prepare the chili. Cut off the stalk end, slice the chili in half and remove the pith and seeds from the center. Chop the chili as finely as possible. Sort through the crabmeat and remove any shell. Cut the bamboo shoots into thin slices and blanch them in lightly salted boiling water for 2 minutes, then drain.

Heat the oil in a wok and stir-fry the ginger, onion and bamboo shoots for 1 minute. Stir in the crab and as much of the chili as you like, and fry for a further 1 minute. Stir in the vinegar, sugar and fish stock and cook for 5 minutes over gentle heat. Thicken by adding the cornstarch paste, stirring continuously until boiling. Season to taste with salt and pepper, garnish with chopped chives and serve.

SEAFOOD COMBINATION

*Using shrimp, flounders and squid for this seafood
combination gives an excellent variety of fishy textures to the
dish. Cod, haddock, plaice or any white fish is suitable.*

Serves 4

INGREDIENTS
1 tbsp dry white wine
½ tsp salt
1 egg white
1 tsp grated fresh root ginger
1 tsp cornstarch
1⅓ cups medium-size shrimp,
   shelled and de-veined
¼ pound flounder fillets, cut into
   1-inch cubes
1 cup snow peas
¼ pound squid tubes, cut into
   1-inch rings
Oil for deep-frying
1 carrot, cut into matchsticks
1 stick celery, sliced diagonally

Combine the wine, salt, egg
white, grated ginger and
cornstarch in a bowl and mix
well. Add the shrimp and fish,
coat evenly and thoroughly, then
drain, reserving the sauce.
Blanch the snow peas in boiling
water for 1 minute and drain.
Open up the squid rings and
score each one with a sharp
knife into a lattice pattern.

Heat the oil in a wok. Deep-fry
the shrimp, fish and squid for 2
minutes. Remove from the wok
using a slotted spoon and drain
on paper towels. Carefully pour
off all but 1 tbsp of oil from the
wok. Heat the oil again and stir-
fry the carrot and celery for 3
minutes. Add the snow peas and
stir-fry for a further 3 minutes.
Add any remaining sauce and
stir. Add the seafood and toss
well until heated through. Serve
immediately.

QUICK FRIED SHRIMP

This is quick and easy to prepare and requires very little cooking. Use cooked or raw shrimp, adjusting the brief cooking period accordingly.

Serves 4-6

INGREDIENTS

2 pounds cooked shrimp in their shells
2 cloves garlic, crushed
1-inch piece fresh root ginger, peeled and finely chopped
1 tbsp freshly chopped cilantro leaves
3 tbsps oil
1 tbsp rice wine or dry sherry
1½ tbsps light soy sauce
Chopped scallions to garnish

Shell the shrimp except for the tail ends – this gives a most attractive presentation. Place the shrimp in a bowl with the remaining ingredients, except for the garnish, and leave to marinate for 30 minutes. Heat a wok and add the shrimp and their marinade. Stir-fry briefly to heat the shrimp, taking care not to overcook them. Scatter the chopped scallions over the shrimp and serve.

SQUID WITH BROCCOLI & CAULIFLOWER

I adore squid – fried, steamed, stewed in its own ink, any way at all! I was always intrigued about how the Chinese got it to a different shape to everyone else – well, once I started Chinese cooking, I soon found out!

Serves 4

INGREDIENTS

1 pound squid tubes
⅔ cup oil for deep-frying
1 onion, roughly chopped
2 sticks celery, sliced diagonally
½ pound broccoli flowerets
½ pounds cauliflower flowerets
½ tsp grated fresh root ginger
1 tbsp cornstarch
2 tbsps water
2 tbsps light soy sauce
2 tbsps Chinese wine or dry
  sherry
2 tbsps oyster sauce
½ tsp sesame oil
½ tsp sugar
Salt and freshly ground black
  pepper

Cut the cleaned squid lengthwise down the center. Flatten out with the inside uppermost. With a sharp knife make a lattice design, cutting deep into the squid flesh. This tenderizes the squid and makes it curl during cooking.

Heat the oil in a wok. Add the squid and cook until it curls, then remove it from the wok with a slotted spoon and drain on paper towels. Carefully pour off all but 1 tbsp of oil from the wok. Add the onion, celery, broccoli, cauliflower and ginger, and stir-fry for 3 minutes. Mix the cornstarch to a paste with the water, and add the soy sauce, wine or sherry, oyster sauce, sesame oil, sugar, and salt and pepper. Mix well and add to the wok. Bring to a boil and simmer for 3 minutes, stirring continuously. Return the squid to the wok and cook until heated through. Place in a warm serving dish and serve hot with rice.

SCRAMBLED EGGS WITH CRABMEAT

I have often eaten scrambled eggs laced with a few smoked salmon trimmings. It is delicious. With crabmeat it is even more special.

Serves 4

INGREDIENTS
3 Chinese dried mushrooms, soaked for 15 minutes in warm water
8 eggs, beaten
¼ tsp sesame oil
1 tsp rice wine
1 tbsp soy sauce
⅓ pound crabmeat
Salt and freshly ground black pepper

Cook the mushrooms in boiling, salted water for 15 minutes. Rinse in fresh water and set aside to drain, then slice.

In a large bowl mix together the eggs, sliced mushrooms, sesame oil, rice wine, soy sauce and the crabmeat. Season with salt and pepper. Cook by stirring the eggs over very gentle heat in a non-stick skillet. The eggs will thicken slowly. Serve when cooked to your liking.

SHRIMP & GINGER

I love the flavor of fresh ginger – it is fresh, dramatic and excitingly different. It goes particularly well with shellfish.

Serves 6

INGREDIENTS
2 tbsps oil
1½ pounds peeled shrimp
1-inch piece fresh root ginger,
    peeled and finely chopped
2 cloves of garlic, finely chopped
2-3 scallions, chopped
1 leek, white part only, cut into
    strips
1 cup shucked peas
¾ cup beansprouts
2 tbsps dark soy sauce
1 tsp sugar
Pinch of salt

Heat the oil in a wok and stir-fry the shrimp for 2-3 minutes. Remove the shrimp with a slotted spoon and set aside. Reheat the oil and add the ginger and garlic. Stir quickly, then add the scallions, leek and peas. Stir-fry for 2-3 minutes. Add the beansprouts and shrimp to the cooked vegetables. Stir in the soy sauce, sugar and salt and cook for 2 minutes. Serve immediately.

BROCCOLI WITH OYSTERS

This recipe has a touch of luxury about it and is suitable as part of a meal for a special occasion. Use an old, but sharp, knife to open the oysters – they can be very reluctant!

Serves 4

INGREDIENTS
1½ pounds broccoli
8 large oysters
1¼ cups fish stock
1 tsp chopped fresh root ginger
1 sprig fresh thyme
1 tbsp oyster sauce
1 tsp cornstarch, combined with
  a little water
Salt and freshly ground black
  pepper

Choose fresh, green broccoli. Cut off the tough stalks, trim and rinse well. Cook the broccoli in boiling, lightly salted water, until tender but still crispy. Refresh by plunging into cold water and set aside to drain.

Open the oyster shells, cut out and set aside the oysters, and discard both juice and shell. Heat the fish stock and add the ginger, thyme and broccoli. Cook, covered, for 5 minutes. Remove the broccoli with a slotted spoon and add the oysters. Poach them for 1 minute, then remove with a slotted spoon and place on a hot serving dish. Stir the oyster sauce into the fish stock, remove the thyme and stir in the cornstarch paste. Cook until boiling and thickened, then adjust the seasoning as necessary. Serve the oysters surrounded by the broccoli and accompanied by the sauce.

SHRIMP WITH VEGETABLES

A quick dish which will serve four as part of a Chinese meal, or one or two as a supper dish.

Serves 4

INGREDIENTS
½ cucumber
1 cup beansprouts
8 Chinese dried black
   mushrooms, soaked in warm
   water for 15 minutes
2 tbsps peanut oil
1 clove garlic, chopped
1 tsp sugar
1 tsp oyster sauce
1 tsp white wine vinegar
Salt and freshly ground black
   pepper
1 tsp oil
20 shrimp, shelled and de-veined
2 tbsps cornstarch
1 tbsp soy sauce
1 tbsp sesame oil

Peel the cucumber and cut into fine strips. Rinse and drain the beansprouts. Drain the mushrooms and cook in boiling, salted water for 15 minutes. Rinse and set aside to drain again.

Heat the peanut oil in a wok and stir-fry the garlic, beansprouts and mushrooms for 1 minute. Add the cucumber, sugar, oyster sauce, vinegar, salt and pepper. Cook for 2 minutes, stirring continuously. Heat the remaining oil in a skillet. Toss the shrimp in the cornstarch and fry until cooked. Transfer the vegetables to a serving platter. Top with the fried shrimp. Sprinkle with soy sauce and sesame oil and serve immediately.

SWEET & SOUR SHELLFISH

This recipe uses clams but, as the name suggests, any shellfish could be cooked in this way. Mussels, shrimp, squid rings – you choose! Do try not to overcook the shellfish – they easily become tough.

Serves 4

INGREDIENTS

20 clams, rinsed in plenty of running water
⅔ cup Chinese wine
1 tbsp oil
1 tsp finely chopped fresh root ginger
1-2 cloves garlic, finely chopped
½ red pepper, de-seeded and cut into thin matchsticks
½ green pepper, de-seeded and cut into thin matchsticks
¼ cucumber, peeled and cut into thin matchsticks
1 tbsp soy sauce
2 tbsps pineapple or orange juice
1 tsp white wine vinegar
Salt and freshly ground black pepper

Put the clams in a large saucepan, pour in the wine, cover, and place over high heat to open the shells – this should take approximately 3-5 minutes. Remove the pan from the heat and the clams from their shells. Pour the cooking liquid through a very fine sifter and reserve. Keep the shells to one side.

Heat the oil in a wok and stir-fry the ginger, garlic, vegetables and clams for 2 minutes. Stir in the soy sauce, ¼ cup of the reserved cooking liquid, the pineapple or orange juice, and the vinegar. Season with salt and pepper to taste. Cook until the sauce is slightly reduced and the clams are tender. Replace the cooked clams, with the sauce, in the shells. Warm in a hot oven for 2 minutes if necessary and serve immediately.

BREADED SHRIMP WITH FRESH TOMATO SALAD

Combining fried shrimp with a fresh tomato salad is fresh, simple and memorable. Always skin tomatoes from the flower end – it's much easier that way!

Serves 4

INGREDIENTS
5 ripe tomatoes
1 tsp finely chopped fresh root ginger
1 tbsp freshly chopped chives
Salt and freshly ground black pepper
24 fresh shrimp
2 tbsps oil
2 tbsps all-purpose flour
2 eggs, beaten
¼ cup fresh breadcrumbs
1 tsp finely chopped chives for garnish (optional)

Plunge the tomatoes into a bowl of boiling water for 15 seconds. Rinse immediately in cold water and let cool. Skin, de-seed and finely chop the tomatoes. Mix the ginger and chives with the tomatoes. Season and marinate for 2 hours in the refrigerator. Shell the shrimp, leaving their tails on.

Heat the oil in a skillet or wok. Dredge the shrimp in the flour, then dip them in the beaten egg, and finally coat them in the breadcrumbs. Fry until golden in the hot oil. Serve the fried shrimp on a bed of chilled tomato salad, garnished with chopped chives, if wished.

TRIPLE FRY OF "THREE SEA FLAVORS"

I usually advise against using frozen scallops as they collapse when defrosted. However, as the three types of shellfish in this recipe are finely chopped, frozen scallops are fine.

Serves 3-4

INGREDIENTS
1 cup large peeled shrimp
4 scallops
¼ pound squid tubes
1 tbsp salted black beans
2 slices fresh root ginger, peeled
2 scallions
2 cloves garlic
1 small red pepper, de-seeded
⅓ cup oil
½ cup chicken stock
1 tbsp soy sauce
1 tbsp chili sauce
1 tbsp cornstarch blended with 3 tsps water
1½ tsps sesame oil
1 tbsp sherry
Salt and freshly ground black pepper

Finely chop the shrimp, scallops and squid. Soak the black beans in warm water for 5 minutes, then drain and chop them finely. Shred the root ginger, cut the scallions into 1-inch pieces and chop the garlic. Cut the red pepper into 1-inch pieces.

Heat ¼ cup of oil in a large skillet or wok, add the chopped seafood and stir-fry quickly for 1-2 minutes. Remove the seafood with a slotted spoon and drain on paper towels. Add the remaining oil, heat, and add the ginger, garlic and black beans. Stir-fry for 1 minute, then add the scallions and pepper with the stock and cook for 1 minute. Add the soy and chili sauces and return the seafood to the wok, stirring to mix. Finally, add the cornstarch paste, the sesame oil and sherry. Bring rapidly to a boil, stirring continuously. Season to taste, then serve.

STEAMED SHRIMP

Don't throw the zucchini peel away — it is an integral part of this dish! The peel is wrapped around the shrimp giving a most attractive pink and green presentation. Use the zucchini flesh in a vegetable stir-fry to serve with the shrimp.

Serves 4

INGREDIENTS
1 tbsp fish sauce
1 tbsp water
1 tbsp wine vinegar
1 tbsp soy sauce
2 tsps sugar
10 freshly chopped mint leaves
1 shallot, chopped
Salt and freshly ground black
   pepper
2 medium-size zucchini
12 fresh shrimp, shelled and
   cleaned

Mix together the fish sauce, water, vinegar, soy sauce, sugar, mint, shallot, salt and pepper. Stir well and set aside for at least 1 hour. Peel the zucchini carefully and cut the peel into long strips. Just before serving time, season the shrimp with plenty of salt and pepper, then roll the strips of zucchini peel around the shrimp and cook them in a Chinese steamer for 5 minutes. Serve the shrimp very hot, accompanied by the sauce.

GINGER SCALLOPS IN OYSTER SAUCE

Take great care not to overcook the scallops as that will make them tough and rubbery. Frozen scallops should only be used in an emergency – they almost disintegrate when defrosted.

Serves 4

INGREDIENTS

1 pound scallops, cleaned, dried on paper towels, and sliced
Salt
2 tbsps vegetable oil
1 inch fresh root ginger, peeled and very thinly sliced
10 scallions, cut diagonally into 1-inch slices
⅓ cup light stock, or ⅓ cup hot water and half a chicken boullion cube

Sauce

1 tbsp oyster sauce
1 tbsp light soy sauce
½ tsp sesame oil
1 tsp cornstarch
Pinch of sugar
1 tsp grated fresh root ginger

Prepare the sauce: combine the oyster sauce, soy sauce, sesame oil, cornstarch, sugar and grated ginger in a bowl and set aside. Sprinkle the scallops with a pinch of salt. Heat a wok and add the oil. Add the sliced ginger and scallions and stir-fry gently for 1 minute, then turn the heat up to high. Add the scallops and stir-fry for 1 minute, then stir in the sauce mixture. Remove the wok from the heat and gradually add the stock. Return to the heat and bring to a boil, stirring continuously. Simmer gently for 3 minutes, until the sauce is slightly thickened. Adjust the seasoning, then serve immediately with boiled rice.

BOK CHOY WITH OYSTERS

Are oysters a flavor or a funny sensation? Eaten raw they may be the latter, but cooked in this way with vegetables they are wonderful.

Serves 4

INGREDIENTS
12 large oysters
1 pound Bok Choy
1 tbsp oil
1⅓ cups diced bacon
¼ cup fish stock
Salt and freshly ground black
  pepper

Use large oysters if possible. If you have to use smaller ones, increase the number accordingly. Open the oysters, taking care to protect your hand by wrapping a dish cloth around the oysters – the shells are sharp! Cut the oysters away from the shell, reserving the juice. Shred the Bok Choy.

Heat the oil in a wok and stir-fry the bacon. Stir the Bok Choy into the wok and add the fish stock. Check the seasoning, adding salt and pepper to taste. Continue cooking until the Bok Choy is the way you like it. Place the oysters and their juice on top of the Bok choy and poach for approximately 2 minutes. Remove the oysters and place on a hot serving plate. Serve immediately, with the cooked Bok Choy.

HONEY SESAME SHRIMP

These delicious shrimp make a splendid fish course with just a little salad garnish and lots of fresh lemon to squeeze over them. You could trickle a little hot chili sauce over them if you like.

Serves 4

INGREDIENTS

1 cup self-rising flour
Salt and freshly ground black
    pepper
1 egg, lightly beaten
⅔ cup water
1 pound shrimp, shelled and de-
    veined
2 tbsps cornstarch
Oil for deep-frying
1 tbsp sesame oil
2 tbsps honey
1 tbsp sesame seeds

Sift the flour, salt and pepper into a bowl. Make a well in the center and add the egg and water. Mix well, gradually bringing in the flour. Beat to a smooth batter and set aside for 10 minutes. Meanwhile, toss the shrimp in the cornstarch to coat well. Shake off any excess cornstarch. Carefully stir the shrimp into the batter and coat them thoroughly.

Heat the oil in a wok and add the shrimp, a few at a time. Cook until the batter is golden, then remove the shrimp with a slotted spoon. Drain on paper towels and keep warm. Repeat until all the shrimp have been fried.

Carefully pour the hot oil from the wok. Add the sesame oil and heat gently, then add the honey and stir until well mixed and heated through. Add the shrimp to the mixture and toss well. Sprinkle with sesame seeds and toss again. Serve immediately.

SCALLOPS WITH ASPARAGUS

In any cuisine the combination of scallops and asparagus means summer! Here are two tastes that really belong to sunshine and lazy days – this recipe is ideal for such occasions as it is quick to prepare.

Serves 4

INGREDIENTS
16 scallops
16 green asparagus spears
1 tbsp oil

Dipping Sauce
1 tbsp soy sauce
2 tsps sugar
½ scallion, finely chopped
1 tbsp oil
1 tsp wine vinegar
Salt and freshly ground black
  pepper

Prise the scallops open with the point of a sharp knife and extract the scallop and the coral. Rinse well and let dry on a clean dish cloth. Boil the asparagus in salted water until tender, and refresh in cold water. Drain, and cut in half lengthwise, if the spears are large.

Make the dipping sauce by combining the soy sauce, sugar, scallion, oil, vinegar and salt and pepper to taste. Brush the scallops and corals with oil and season them with salt and pepper. Either shallow-fry in oil in a skillet or broil quickly, turning the scallops carefully. Cook for 1 minute on each side. Serve the scallops with the asparagus to dip in the sauce.

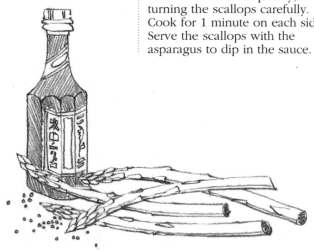

STIR-FRIED SHRIMP & SNOW PEAS

Shrimp and snow peas both have delicate flavors and sometimes it is good to let them shine through without strong spices to mask them. I like to serve this with thread egg noodles.

Serves 4

INGREDIENTS

1 cup snow peas, trimmed
¼ cup peanut oil
½ pound shrimp, shelled and de-
  veined
2 tbsps dry white wine
Juice of half a lemon
1 tbsp light soy sauce
Salt and freshly ground black
  pepper
Parsley to garnish

Blanch the snow peas in boiling salted water for 1 minute, then drain and set aside. Heat a wok, add the peanut oil, and stir-fry the shrimp for 30 seconds. Add the snow peas, dry white wine, lemon juice, soy sauce, and a little salt and pepper. Toss together until heated through. Season to taste and garnish with parsley. Serve immediately with boiled rice.

STIR-FRIED LOBSTER WITH GINGER

I have to confess that lobster often manages not to impress me, especially when served cold. Served hot and flavored with ginger it is delicious.

Serves 4

INGREDIENTS

2 cooked lobsters, each weighing ¾ pound
1 zucchini
1 tbsp oil
2 tsps chopped fresh root ginger
1 tbsp oyster sauce
½ cup fish stock
Salt and freshly ground black pepper
1 tsp cornstarch, combined with a little water

Shell the lobsters and remove the flesh (or buy ready-prepared lobsters). Slice into bite-size pieces. Slice the zucchini thinly.

Heat the oil in a wok and stir-fry the ginger. Add the zucchini and cook until tender but still firm, then add the lobster and heat through. Pour in the oyster sauce and the fish stock. Season with salt and pepper to taste. Let the sauce reduce and thicken slightly. Add the cornstarch paste and cook, stirring continuously, until thickened. Serve immediately.

CHICKEN & DUCK

Chicken and duck are the most widely eaten poultry in China, although pigeon and quail are also popular and some geese are prepared for the table. It is impossible to know even a little about Chinese food without realizing that crispy duck and chicken are among the most popular dishes in the Chinese cuisine.

A Good Mixer

Chicken is the most highly prized, as well as the most widely used, of all poultry in China. It is eaten daily in the homes of the affluent but they seldom tire of it as it is so versatile and can be prepared in literally hundreds of ways. Chicken has

quite a light, mild flavor and therefore absorbs seasonings readily, making it a good mixer with many different vegetables. It also blends well with shrimp and other shellfish in dishes such as fried rice and mixed chop suey.

What, No Oven?

It seems surprising but, even now, most homes in China do not have an oven – you will find that very few recipes in this book require an oven and that almost all the food is cooked by stir-frying, steaming, dry-frying or braising (that is, braising in a pan rather than in the oven). It is therefore very unusual to find a recipe for chicken which requires roasting; to achieve such a result in China you would have to make friends with the local restaurateur, who might have an oven.

Pluck Your Own

The love of fine cuisine is deeply rooted in the Chinese culture and, perhaps because of this, they are far less squeamish about killing, plucking and dressing their poultry than many of us who are used to buying it "oven-ready." This creates much more work for the cook but does ensure that the poultry is as fresh as possible, with all the benefit of flavor that this brings. The French, who are also admired for their food, have a similar attitude to fresh poultry and in both China and France it is very common to see live chickens in cages in the markets.

If you do not want to pursue the traditions of classic Chinese cuisine to the extent of plucking your own poultry, the next best flavor will be achieved by using free-range or corn-fed chickens, both of which are now easy to come by both in supermarkets and in smaller shops.

An All-round Winner

Chicken is so versatile. It can be cooked in many different ways, even when the cooking is limited to a burner, and mixed with almost every ingredient. It can be flavored with the mildest of seasonings and steamed to maximize the natural flavor of the chicken; and it can withstand the boldest of treatments with chilis, peppers and any of the hottest sauces. It is most practical (and economical) to buy a whole chicken and to joint it yourself, which will provide a variety of meats for a variety of dishes – remember, most Chinese recipes use comparatively little meat, combining it with vegetables to make the meat go further. And don't discard the bones; use them for stock and for so many of the Chinese soups.

Peking Duck – a Brand New Classic

Peking Duck is probably the most famous of all Chinese recipes. It would be more than reasonable to assume that the origins of the dish must be almost lost in history, but this is not so. For one thing, Peking Duck is roasted and, as I have said before, very few homes in China have an oven! So, this great dish was originally only to be found in restaurants and then only from the latter half of the nineteenth century. It is said to have originated not in Peking at all, but in Inner Mongolia! Well, whatever the history, it is the most delicious of dishes!

What makes Peking Duck so exceptional amongst duck dishes is its crispy skin. This, in my opinion, makes it stand out from all other duck dishes, Chinese or otherwise.

There are many recipes for duck which sound very similar. The difference is in the preparation and the seasoning of the meat. Sometimes duck is marinated before cooking, and sometimes it is steamed before frying. Interestingly enough, fried duck sounds as if it should be very greasy, but it is not at all – the frying takes place at such a high temperature that the duck meat is very crispy but dry once cooking is complete.

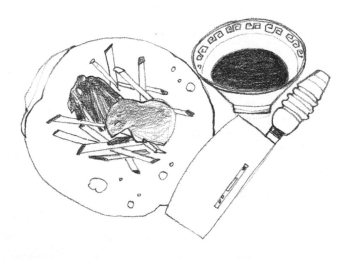

SZECHUAN BANG BANG CHICKEN

Bang Bang Chicken should be served in layers from a platter. Everyone should toss their individual helping to mix all the ingredients together before eating.

Serves 4

INGREDIENTS
2 chicken breasts
1 medium cucumber

Sauce
¼ cup peanut butter
2 tsps sesame oil
½ tsp sugar
¼ tsp salt
2 tsps stock
½ tsp chili sauce

Simmer the chicken breasts in a pan of water for 30 minutes, then drain and cut them into ½-inch thick slices. Slice the cucumber thinly, or cut it into sticks. Make a bed of it on a large serving platter. Pile the shredded chicken on top. Mix the peanut butter with the sesame oil, sugar, salt and stock. Pour the sauce evenly over the chicken and trickle the chili sauce over it.

SZECHUAN CHILI CHICKEN

The Szechuan-style heat in this recipe comes from the dried and fresh chilies – use half quantities of both if you think the dish might be too hot!

Serves 4

INGREDIENTS
¾ pound boneless chicken
   breasts
1 tsp salt
1 egg white
⅓ cup oil
1½ tbsps cornstarch
2 slices fresh root ginger, peeled
2 small dried chilies
2 green or red peppers, de-
   seeded
2 fresh chilies, de-seeded and
   finely chopped
2 tbsps soy sauce
2 tbsps wine vinegar

Cut the chicken into bite-size pieces. Add the salt, egg white, 1 tbsp oil, and the cornstarch. Rub the seasoning evenly over the chicken pieces to form a thin coating.

Chop the ginger and dried chilies and cut the peppers into bite-size pieces. Heat the remaining oil in a wok. Add the ginger and the fresh and dried chilies and stir-fry for 1 minute. Add the chicken pieces, separating them while stirring. Cook until lightly browned. Add the peppers, soy sauce and vinegar and fry for a further 2 minutes. Serve immediately with steamed rice.

STIR-FRIED CHICKEN ON CRISPY NOODLES

This spicy chicken stir-fry is ideal for serving with crispy noodles. Some supermarkets sell ground turkey, which could be used in place of the chicken, but it is not so authentic.

Serves 4

INGREDIENTS
½ pound chicken breasts
2 slices cooked smoked ham
6 slices fresh root ginger, peeled
1 large onion
3 scallions
3 tbsps oil
½ tsp salt
2 tbsps soy sauce
2 tbsps chicken stock
1 tbsp vinegar
1 tbsp sherry
1 tbsp chili oil
1 tsp sugar
2 tsps cornstarch
2 tbsps water

Chop the chicken finely. Shred the ham, ginger and onion finely, and slice the scallions. Heat the oil in a large skillet or wok. Add the onion, ham and ginger and stir-fry for 2 minutes. Add the chicken, sprinkle with salt, soy sauce and stock, then stir-fry for a further 2 minutes. Add the vinegar, sherry, chili oil, sugar, and scallions. Blend the cornstarch with 2 tbsps water and add to the mixture. Cook over high heat for 2 minutes until boiling and thickened.

CHICKEN WITH BEANSPROUTS

The marinade which flavors the chicken provides the base for this dish of chicken and beansprouts.

Serves 4

INGREDIENTS
1 chicken
1 tbsp Chinese wine
1 tsp cornstarch
1 cup beansprouts
2 tbsps oil
½ scallion, finely sliced
1 tsp sugar
1¼ cups chicken stock
Salt and freshly ground black
  pepper

Bone the chicken and cut the meat into thin slices or strips. Place the chicken on a plate and pour the Chinese wine over it. Sprinkle with the cornstarch and stir well. Leave the chicken to marinate for 30 minutes.

Blanch the beansprouts in lightly salted boiling water for 1 minute. Rinse under cold running water and set aside to drain. Remove the chicken from the marinade with a slotted spoon.

Heat the oil in a wok and stir-fry the scallion and the chicken until browned. Add the drained beansprouts and the sugar, then stir in the marinade and the stock. Let the chicken cook through, which will take approximately 20 minutes. Check the seasoning, adding salt and pepper to taste. Serve immediately.

DEEP-FRIED CHICKEN
WITH LEMON SLICES

*There are many variations on the recipe of Lemon Chicken.
In this recipe the chicken is marinated and fried before
being added to a lemon sauce.*

Serves 6-8

INGREDIENTS
3 pounds boneless chicken
  breasts
⅓ cup cornstarch
3 tbsps all-purpose flour
1 green pepper, de-seeded
1 red pepper, de-seeded
Oil for deep-frying
2 lemons, thinly sliced
Freshly chopped parsley

Chicken Marinade
½ tsp salt
½ tsp white wine
2 tsps light soy sauce
1 tbsp cornstarch
1 tbsp water
1 egg yolk
Freshly ground black pepper

Sauce
3 tbsps sugar
3 tbsps lemon juice
⅓ cup chicken or vegetable stock
½ tsp salt
2 tbsps cornstarch
1 tsp sesame oil

Skin the chicken breasts and cut them into thin, bite-size pieces. Mix together all the ingredients for the marinade, add the prepared chicken and leave for 10 minutes. Mix the cornstarch and flour together on a plate and use to coat the chicken pieces. Combine the ingredients for the sauce in a small bowl. Cut the peppers into 1-inch pieces.

Place a wok over high heat, add the oil and heat until almost smoking. Deep-fry the chicken slices until golden brown. Remove with a slotted spoon to a heated plate. Pour off all but 1 tbsp of the oil. Stir-fry the peppers until they begin to brown, then add the sauce. Bring to a boil, stirring until thickened. Add the chicken pieces, and stir for a further few minutes. Transfer to a heated serving platter, and garnish with the lemon slices and chopped parsley.

STIR-FRIED CHICKEN WITH YELLOW BEAN SAUCE

Yellow Bean Sauce is one of the many stir-fry sauces available in supermarkets. It is quite salty but not as strong in flavor as some other Chinese sauces. Specialist Chinese shops may offer a whole bean or a crushed bean sauce; supermarkets usually stock the latter.

Serves 4

INGREDIENTS
1 egg white, lightly beaten
1 tbsp cornstarch
Salt and freshly ground black
    pepper
1 pound boneless chicken
    breasts, thinly sliced
1 tbsp rice vinegar
1 tbsp light soy sauce
1 tsp sugar
2 tbsps oil
2 tbsps yellow bean sauce
Scallion flowers (see recipe for
    Barbecued Spareribs) to
    garnish

Mix the lightly beaten egg white with the cornstarch and a little salt and pepper. Place the sliced chicken in a bowl and pour the egg mixture over, tossing the chicken until well coated. Set aside in a cool place for at least 1 hour.

Combine the vinegar, soy sauce and sugar in a bowl. Remove the chicken to a plate with a slotted spoon and set the egg mixture aside.

Heat a wok and add the oil. When hot, stir-fry the chicken until lightly browned, then remove it from the wok. Add the yellow bean sauce to the wok and stir-fry for 1 minute, then add the vinegar mixture and stir well. Return the chicken to the wok, and cook gently for 2 minutes. Finally, add the egg mixture and simmer until the sauce boils and thickens, stirring all the time. Garnish with scallion flowers. Serve immediately with boiled rice.

BRAISED CHICKEN WITH GINGER

I always think of braising as a cooking process in the oven, but the Oriental way is in a pan of stock with the vegetables in the base of the pan. It works well, as you will see.

Serves 4

INGREDIENTS
1 chicken, boned
½ tsp chopped fresh root ginger
1 carrot, peeled and diced
1 turnip, peeled and diced
1 zucchini, diced
1 onion, thinly sliced
5 slices fresh root ginger, peeled
Salt and freshly ground black
  pepper

Separate the breasts and the leg meat from the boned chicken. Keep each leg in one piece. Place the remaining meat and the bones from the chicken in a saucepan, with just enough water to cover. Boil until the liquid has reduced to a quarter. Pour the stock through a fine strainer.

Sprinkle the chopped ginger on the inside of the 2 pieces of chicken leg meat and season with salt and pepper. Roll up tightly and fasten with kitchen string.

Add ⅔ cup water to the chicken stock and bring to a boil in a saucepan. Add the prepared vegetables, sliced ginger, rolled leg meat and the 2 chicken breasts. Cook for approximately 35 minutes or until the chicken is cooked through. Remove the rolled leg meat, cut off the string and cut the meat into circles. Spread the slices on a warmed serving plate. Take out the chicken breasts and slice them thinly. Arrange the slices on the warmed plate with the leg meat. Remove the vegetables using a slotted spoon, arrange them around the meat and then pour over a little of the stock. Serve very hot.

CHICKEN LIVERS WITH PEPPERS

The Chinese eat a great deal of chicken and would certainly not waste the livers. This recipe is mild in flavor and could be spiced by adding a pinch of five-spice powder.

Serves 4

INGREDIENTS
4 Chinese dried mushrooms
1 pound chicken livers
1-inch piece fresh root ginger
1 tbsp rice vinegar
2 tsps sugar
1 small leek
1 onion
1 green pepper
1 red pepper
3 tbsps vegetable oil
2 scallion flowers (see recipe for Barbecued Spareribs) to garnish

Soak the mushrooms in hot water for 20 minutes. Trim the chicken livers. Blanch them in boiling water for 3 minutes, then drain and slice. Peel and slice the root ginger finely.

Mix together the vinegar and sugar, add the ginger and set aside. Clean and trim the leek and cut into thin rings or slices. Peel and slice the onion and cut into strips, then de-seed the peppers, cutting them also into strips. Drain the mushrooms and remove the hard stalks, then cut the caps into thin slices.

Heat a wok. Add the oil and, when hot, add the mushrooms, onion, leek and peppers. Stir-fry for 5 minutes. Remove the vegetables with a slotted spoon and set aside. Add the sliced livers and ginger mixture to the wok and stir-fry for 5 minutes. Return the vegetables to the wok and heat through. Serve garnished with the scallion flowers.

LEMON CHICKEN

Lemon Chicken is one of my favorite Oriental dishes – no package mix can ever equal the exquisite flavor of a homemade sauce! I serve it with broccoli and snow peas, stir-fried and sprinkled with sesame seeds.

Serves 4

INGREDIENTS
⅓ cup oil for frying
2 pounds chicken pieces
Lemon slices to garnish

Lemon Sauce
1 tbsp cornstarch
⅓ cup water
Juice of 1 lemon
2 tbsps sweet sherry
Pinch of sugar, if required

Heat a wok and add the oil. When hot, add the chicken pieces and turn them in the oil until well browned. Lower the heat, cover and simmer for 30 minutes, or until the chicken is cooked. Remove the chicken with a slotted spoon and drain on paper towels. Place the chicken pieces in a serving dish and keep them warm in the oven.

Prepare the sauce. Carefully drain the oil from the wok. Mix the cornstarch to a paste with 2 tbsps of the water. Place the lemon juice and remaining water in the wok, and bring to a boil. Add the cornstarch, and stir until boiling, then simmer for 2 minutes until thickened. Add the sherry and sugar, and simmer for a further 2 minutes. Pour the sauce over the chicken pieces and garnish with lemon slices. Serve with boiled rice.

CHICKEN & CASHEWS

Cashew nuts may seem to be a really luxurious ingredient, but they are quite commonplace in Chinese cooking. In this recipe they retain some of their crunchy texture and contrast well with the tender pieces of chicken.

Serves 4

INGREDIENTS

1 pound chicken breasts,
   skinned, boned and shredded
⅔ cup chicken stock *or* ⅔ cup
   hot water and 1 chicken
   boullion cube
¼ cup cornstarch
½ tsp five-spice powder
Salt
¼ cup peanut oil
1 onion, sliced
1 clove garlic, crushed
1 stick celery, thinly sliced
¼ pound green beans, trimmed
   and sliced
1 carrot, cut into matchsticks
2 scallions, sliced
1 tbsp light soy sauce
½ cup roasted cashews

Simmer the chicken bones in a little water to make chicken stock, or dissolve the chicken boullion cube in hot water. Set aside to cool. Combine half the cornstarch, the five-spice powder and a pinch of salt, then toss the shredded chicken in the mixture.

Heat a wok and add the peanut oil. When hot, add the chicken pieces, a few at a time, tossing them in the hot oil. Stir-fry for about 3 minutes until the chicken starts to change color. Remove the chicken with a slotted spoon, and drain on paper towels. Repeat until all the chicken is cooked. Carefully pour off all but 1 tbsp of oil. Add the onion and garlic, then cook for 2 minutes. Add the celery, beans, carrot and scallions, and stir-fry for a further 2 minutes. Strain the chicken stock into the wok and cook for 3 minutes, until the vegetables are tender but still crispy. Mix the remaining cornstarch with 2 tbsps of water, add the soy sauce and pour the mixture into the wok. Adjust the seasoning if necessary. Return to a boil and let the mixture simmer for 3 minutes. Add the chicken and heat through.

Remove the wok from the heat. Stir in the cashews, and serve at once with noodles or rice.

PEKING EGG BATTERED CHICKEN WITH BEANSPROUTS, IN ONION AND GARLIC SAUCE

Serve this dish with plain boiled rice and some broccoli stir-fried with other seasonal vegetables. The beansprouts should be cooked very briefly, so that they remain crispy.

Serves 4

INGREDIENTS
3 boneless chicken breasts
Salt and freshly ground black
  pepper
2 eggs, lightly beaten
2 cloves garlic
2 scallions
¼ cup oil
¼ cup chicken stock
Vinegar to taste
1 cup beansprouts

Cut each chicken breast into very thin 4-inch slices and rub them with salt and pepper. Beat the eggs lightly, and add the chicken slices. Crush the garlic and cut the scallions into 1-inch pieces.

Heat the oil in a wok. Add the chicken pieces one by one, then lower the heat. Leave to cook for 1-2 minutes. Once the egg coating has set, sprinkle the chicken with garlic and scallions. Finally, add the stock and vinegar to taste, then simmer gently for 2 minutes.

Remove the chicken from the wok and cut each slice into small even-size pieces. Pour the remaining sauce from the wok over the chicken. Add the beansprouts to the empty wok, toss in any remaining sauce and stir-fry briefly – for a few seconds. Make a bed of beansprouts on a warmed serving platter. Serve the chicken in the onion and garlic sauce on top.

STIR-FRIED CHICKEN WITH SLICED ZUCCHINI

This chicken recipe is very lightly flavored and is served in a clear cornstarch glaze on a bed of fried zucchini slices.

Serves 4-6

INGREDIENTS

1½ pounds boneless chicken
   breasts
2 tsps cornstarch
1 egg white
1 tbsp pale dry sherry
1 tsp salt
¼ tsp freshly ground black
   pepper
½ pound zucchini
¼ cup peanut oil
2 slices fresh root ginger, peeled
   and shredded

Cut the chicken into thin slices. In a large bowl, mix the chicken with the cornstarch, egg white, sherry, salt and pepper. Leave for a few minutes, then drain, reserving the marinade. Cut the zucchini into thin slices.

Heat 3 tbsps of the oil in a wok with the ginger. Add the chicken, and stir-fry for 2 minutes, until all the pieces have turned white. Transfer the chicken to a bowl. Wipe the wok clean and add the remaining peanut oil, then stir-fry the zucchini for 2 minutes. Transfer them to a serving platter. Return the chicken to the wok, add the cornstarch mixture and stir for a few seconds until boiling, resulting in a clear glaze. Pour the contents of the wok into the middle of the zucchini. Serve at once.

CHICKEN LIVERS WITH BOK CHOY & ALMONDS

Chicken livers require only light flavorings and seasonings, which will not mask their own delicate flavor. The crunchy texture of the fried almonds contrasts well with the soft, moist livers.

Serves 4

INGREDIENTS
½ pound chicken livers
3 tbsps oil
¼ cup split blanched almonds
1 clove garlic
½ cup snow peas
8-10 Bok Choy leaves, finely
    shredded
2 tsps cornstarch mixed with 1
    tbsp cold water
2 tbsps soy sauce
⅔ cup chicken stock

Sort through the chicken livers and remove any discolored areas or tubes. Cut the livers into even-size pieces. Heat a wok and pour in the oil. When the oil is hot, turn the heat down and add the almonds. Cook over gentle heat, stirring continuously, until golden brown. Remove the almonds and drain on paper towels.

Add the garlic to the wok. Cook for 1-2 minutes to flavor the oil, then remove the garlic and discard. Add the chicken livers and cook for about 2-3 minutes, stirring frequently. Remove the livers and set aside. Add the snow peas to the wok and stir-fry for 1 minute. Add the Bok Choy and cook for 1 minute. Remove the vegetables and set them aside. Mix the cornstarch and water with the soy sauce and stock. Pour into the wok and bring to a boil. Cook until thickened and clear. Return all the other ingredients to the sauce and reheat for 30 seconds. Serve immediately.

CHICKEN WITH WALNUTS & CELERY

Oyster sauce is one of my favorite strong Chinese flavorings. The addition of walnuts to this stir-fry makes an unusual dish.

Serves 4

INGREDIENTS
½ pound boneless chicken, cut into 1-inch pieces
2 tbsps soy sauce
2 tsps brandy
1 tsp cornstarch
Salt and freshly grated black pepper
2 tbsps oil
1 clove garlic
⅔ cup walnut halves
3 sticks celery, cut in diagonal slices
2 tsps oyster sauce
⅔ cup water or chicken stock

Combine the chicken with the soy sauce, brandy, cornstarch, salt and pepper. Heat a wok and add the oil and garlic. Cook for about 1 minute to flavor the oil, then remove the garlic and discard. Add half the chicken and stir-fry quickly without letting it turn brown. Remove the chicken, then add the other half of it and cook as before. Remove the cooked chicken. Add the walnuts to the wok and cook for about 2 minutes, until lightly browned and crispy. Add the celery to the wok and cook for about 1 minute. Add the oyster sauce and water and bring to a boil. When boiling, return the chicken to the pan and stir to coat all the ingredients well. Serve immediately.

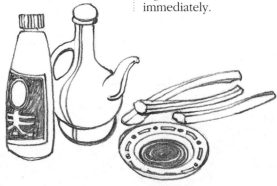

CHICKEN WITH CLOUD EARS

Chinese mushrooms have wonderful names! Unless you can get to a Chinese supermarket you may have difficulty buying specific varieties of dried Oriental mushrooms, but any type may be used for this recipe.

Serves 4

INGREDIENTS

12 cloud ears, wood ears or other Chinese dried mushrooms, soaked in boiling water for 5 minutes
1 pound chicken breasts, boned and thinly sliced
1 egg white
3 tsps cornstarch
2 tsps white wine
2 tsps sesame oil
1-inch piece fresh root ginger, peeled and left whole
1 clove garlic, left whole
1¼ cups oil
1¼ cups chicken stock
3 tbsps light soy sauce
Salt and freshly ground black pepper

Soak the mushrooms until they soften and swell. Remove all the skin and bone from the chicken and cut the meat into thin slices. Mix the chicken with the egg white, 2 tsps cornstarch, wine and sesame oil. Heat a wok for a few minutes, then pour in the oil for frying. Add the whole piece of ginger and whole garlic clove to the oil and cook for about 1 minute. Remove and discard the ginger and garlic. Lower the heat. Add about a quarter of the chicken at a time to the wok and stir-fry each batch for 1 minute. Remove the cooked pieces and continue cooking the rest until all the chicken is fried.

Remove all but 2 tbsps of the oil from the wok. Drain the mushrooms and squeeze them to extract all the liquid. If using mushrooms with stems, remove and discard the stems before slicing the caps thinly. Cut cloud ears or wood ears into small pieces. Add the mushrooms to the wok and cook for about 1 minute, then add the stock and let it come almost to a boil. Mix the remaining cornstarch and the soy sauce and add a spoonful of the hot stock to it. Add the mixture to the wok, stirring constantly, and bring to a boil. Let boil for 1-2 minutes or until thickened. The sauce will clear when the cornstarch has cooked sufficiently. Return the chicken to the wok and add salt and pepper. Stir thoroughly for about 1 minute and serve immediately.

CHICKEN IN
HOT PEPPER SAUCE

You can make this sauce as hot as you like by simply adding more chili sauce. Taste after each addition – you can always add more, but you can never take any away!

Serves 4

INGREDIENTS
1 chicken
2 tbsps oil
2-3 cloves garlic, chopped
1 green pepper, de-seeded and cut into thin strips
1 red pepper, de-seeded and cut into thin strips
1 tsp wine vinegar
1 tbsp light soy sauce
1 tsp sugar
1¼ cups chicken stock
1 tbsp chili sauce
Salt and freshly ground black pepper

First bone the chicken completely and cut all the meat into thin strips. Heat the oil in a wok. Stir-fry the garlic, chicken and green and red peppers for about 15 minutes, until the chicken is cooked. Pour off any excess oil and add the vinegar. Boil until almost evaporated, then stir in the soy sauce, sugar and stock. Gradually add the chili sauce, tasting after each addition. Season with a little salt and pepper to taste. Cook until the sauce has reduced slightly. Serve very hot.

CHICKEN BREASTS WITH SCALLION

Steamed chicken is deliciously moist and tender – it is an excellent way of cooking chicken breasts, which can be very dry and slightly tough. The chicken is served with a very lightly flavored sauce made of reduced stock and soy sauce.

Serves 4

INGREDIENTS
1 scallion, sliced
1 carrot, cut into thin strips
2-3 cloves garlic, chopped
4 chicken breasts
Salt and freshly ground black
  pepper
1 cup chicken stock
1 tbsp soy sauce
½ tsp sugar
1 tsp cornstarch, combined with
  a little water

Mix together the scallion, carrot and half the garlic. Slice the chicken breasts open lengthwise, along the side, without cutting through them completely. Season the insides with salt and pepper and fill each breast with ¼ of the vegetable stuffing. Pull the top half of the breast back into place. Season again with salt and pepper. Steam the stuffed chicken breasts for approximately 15 minutes, until cooked through.

Bring the stock to the boil in a small saucepan. Stir in the soy sauce, sugar and the remaining garlic, simmer and allow to reduce for a few minutes. Thicken the sauce by adding the cornstarch paste and stirring continuously until boiling and thickened. Cut the stuffed chicken breasts into slices and serve them topped with sauce.

STUFFED CHICKEN LEGS

*Boning chicken legs is not too difficult a task providing you
have a small, sharp knife. Remove any white sinews as well,
as these are tough and unpleasant to eat. Boneless chicken
thighs may be prepared in the same way, although their
shape will not be quite so neat.*

Serves 4

INGREDIENTS
6-8 Chinese dried black
    mushrooms, soaked for 15
    minutes in warm water
4 chicken legs, boned
1 egg, beaten
½ tsp finely chopped fresh root
    ginger
1¼ cups chicken stock
½ tsp sugar
Salt and freshly ground black
    pepper
1 tsp cornstarch, combined with
    a little water

Drain the mushrooms and cut
them into thin slices. Flatten out
each piece of leg meat and brush
a little beaten egg over the
inside. Divide the mushroom
slices evenly between the 4
pieces of meat and sprinkle with
half the ginger. Roll up and
secure with thin kitchen string.
Steam the stuffed chicken rolls
for approximately 25 minutes, or
until cooked.

Bring the stock to a boil in a pan
and allow to reduce by half. Add
the remaining ginger and the
sugar, and season with salt and
pepper to taste. Add the
cornstarch paste to the sauce,
and heat, stirring continuously,
until boiling and thickened. Serve
the chicken rolls sliced into
rounds and topped with the
sauce.

CHICKEN WITH LEMON & GINGER SAUCE

Using a whole chicken for this recipe is more economical than buying prepared boneless breast fillets. However, if you prefer to buy the fillets you will need 4 pieces, weighing about 1½ pounds in total.

Serves 4

INGREDIENTS
1 lemon, washed
6-8 Chinese dried black
  mushrooms, soaked for 15
  minutes in warm water
2 tbsps oil
1 chicken, boned, the meat cut
  into thin slices
1 tsp chopped fresh root ginger
1 tsp wine vinegar
1 tbsp soy sauce
1¼ cups chicken stock
½ tsp sugar
Salt and freshly ground black
  pepper

Peel the lemon with a potato peeler, and cut the peel into thin strips. Blanch in boiling water for a few seconds and set aside to drain. Squeeze and reserve the juice of the lemon. Cook the mushrooms in lightly salted boiling water for 15 minutes and then rinse them in cold water. Drain the mushrooms thoroughly, and slice them thinly.

Heat the oil in a wok and stir-fry the chicken, ginger and lemon peel for 2 minutes. Pour off any excess fat. Add the vinegar to the wok, heating until it has almost evaporated. Stir in the lemon juice, soy sauce, stock, sugar and mushrooms. Lower the heat and cook for 5 minutes. Season with salt and pepper to taste and serve hot.

PEKING DUCK

This world-famous dish is a particular favorite of mine. Not only do the crispy skin, succulent meat and tangy sauce make a wonderful combination; the messy process of filling the pancakes adds to the enjoyment. Although we tend to eat all the ingredients together, traditionally only the skin was eaten with the pancakes, cucumber and scallions. The duck was carved and served as a second course.

Serves 6

INGREDIENTS
1 duck, weighing 5 pounds

Glaze
⅓ cup maltose (malt sugar) or
    creamed honey
⅓ cup boiling water
1 tbsp soy sauce

Duck Sauce
3 tbsps sesame oil
¾ cup sweet bean paste or
    hoisin sauce
¾ cup sugar
¾ cup water

Mandarin Pancakes (makes 30)
4 cups all-purpose flour
1⅔ cups water
Sesame oil

To serve
1 large cucumber
12 scallions

To prepare the duck, wipe the inside with damp paper towels, but do not wet the skin. Place the duck on a rack in a sink and pour a kettleful of boiling water over it. Pat the duck with ▶

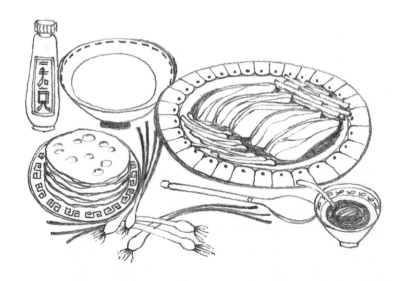

129

paper towels to remove any excess moisture and transfer the duck to another rack over a tray. Mix the glaze ingredients together and brush all over the duck. Coat the inside of the duck as well. Leave the duck to dry for about 1 hour, or until the glaze has dried, then paint with another layer of the glaze and leave to dry again. Repeat until the glaze is used up. If possible, hang the duck on two meat hooks tucked under the wings (otherwise leave the duck on the rack), and leave in a cool airy place overnight (a pantry would be ideal) to allow the skin to dry completely. Do not pierce the skin.

To make the duck sauce, heat the oil in a pan, add the sweet bean paste, sugar and water and mix together until well blended. Simmer for 2-3 minutes, or until the sauce thickens. Pour into a bowl and leave to cool, then chill until required.

To prepare the pancakes, sift the flour into a mixing bowl and make a well in the center. Bring 1¼ cups of the water to a rolling boil and pour into the flour. Quickly stir the flour, a little at a time, into the water, using the handle of a wooden spoon. When well mixed, stir in the rest of the cold water and mix to a dough. Turn out on to a lightly floured surface and knead for 5-6 minutes until the dough is smooth. Cover the dough with plastic wrap and leave to rest for 15-20 minutes.

Knead the dough again for a few more minutes until smooth. Divide into two even-size pieces, then roll each piece out into a long sausage shape and cut into a total of 30 equal pieces. Working with two pieces of dough at a time, roll each piece

into a ball. Keep the rest of the dough covered to prevent it from drying out. Flatten all the dough balls into circles using your hands. Using a pastry brush, paint half the circles with sesame oil on one side. Sandwich the other circles on top of the oiled surfaces to make 15 pairs. Keep each pair as even-sized as possible and, on a lightly floured surface, roll out one pair at a time until they are wafer thin and almost transparent. The circles should be about 6½ inches in diameter. Repeat with the remaining dough.

Heat a heavy-based, non-stick skillet or griddle over medium heat. Wipe the surface with an oiled cloth and place one pair of pancakes in the pan. Cook for 1-2 minutes or until brown spots appear on the underside. Turn the pancakes over and cook the other side until the surface starts to puff up. Remove from the pan and separate the two pancakes while they are still hot. Stack on a plate and keep covered to prevent them from drying out.

To cook the duck, place it on a rack over a roasting pan and roast in the middle of a 375°F oven for 30 minutes. Turn the duck over using two wooden spoons so that you don't pierce the skin, and roast for a further 20 minutes. Turn the duck back over again and continue roasting for 20-30 minutes, or until the skin is dark brown and crispy. If the skin starts to look too brown too soon, lower the oven temperature to 325°F, then raise it to 425°F for the last 10-15 minutes.

While the duck is cooking, cut the cucumber and scallions into thin strips. To reheat the pancakes, place batches in a steamer over boiling water for

5-10 minutes. Alternatively, wait until the duck is cooked and reheat them in the oven.

Remove the duck from the oven and let it stand for 10 minutes before carving. (If wished, the pancakes can now be reheated in the oven, wrapped in foil, at the reduced temperature of 350°F.) Cut the skin into pieces, then carve the meat. Serve with the pancakes, scallions and cucumber and the duck sauce.

DUCK WITH CORIANDER SAUCE

One of the best things about duck, in my opinion, is the crispy skin, so I particularly like recipes such as this which use the skin as a garnish.

Serves 4

INGREDIENTS

1 duck, boned, leg and breast meat reserved (use the bones and remaining meat for stock)
1 scallion
¼ cup bamboo shoots, blanched
2 Chinese dried mushrooms, soaked for 15 minutes in warm water and drained
10 coriander seeds
1¼ cups duck stock
1 tsp cornstarch, combined with a little water
Salt and freshly ground black pepper
3 tbsps oil

Skin the duck breasts and reserve both the meat and skin. Chop the following ingredients separately in a food processor: one duck breast, then the scallion, the bamboo shoots and the Chinese mushrooms. Mix all the processed ingredients together in a small bowl to make stuffing. Spread the stuffing mixture onto the boned leg meat and the remaining duck breast. Roll the meat around the stuffing and wrap each duck parcel in foil. Twist the ends to seal well. Steam the duck rolls in a steamer for 35 minutes.

Crush the coriander seeds and place in a small saucepan. Add the duck stock and cook over gentle heat until reduced by a quarter. Thicken, if necessary, with the cornstarch, stirring continuously until boiling and thickened. Season to taste with salt and pepper. Heat the oil in a skillet and fry the reserved duck skin until crispy. Leave to cool and then cut into small pieces. Remove the foil from the duck. Serve the rolls sliced into circles, with some of the crispy skin and the sauce.

DUCKLING WITH CASHEW NUTS

I love cashew nuts; so I tend to use a few more than the recipe says. I like to cut them quite coarsely, to obtain a crunchy texture. Walnuts or pecan nuts would also work well in this recipe.

Serves 4

INGREDIENTS
20 raw cashew nut halves
2 tbsps oil
2 cloves garlic, finely chopped
1 duckling, boned, the meat cut into slices
1 scallion, chopped
2 tbsps soy sauce
1 cup chicken stock
½ tsp vinegar
1 tsp sugar
Salt and freshly ground black pepper

Slice the cashew nuts into thin strips using a very sharp knife. Heat the oil in a wok and stir-fry the garlic and duckling until the meat is sealed and browned. Add the cashew nuts and the scallion and stir-fry for 1 minute. Pour off any excess fat from the wok. Stir in the soy sauce, then the stock, vinegar and sugar. Season with salt and pepper. Continue cooking until the duckling is tender and the sauce has reduced enough to coat the pieces of meat lightly.

DUCKLING WITH ONIONS

This recipe, which sounds and tastes luxurious, is simple and quick to prepare. The sauce is rich and full of flavor, so serve the duckling with boiled rice and a plain Oriental vegetable stir-fry.

Serves 4

INGREDIENTS
2 tbsps oil
2 large onions, finely sliced
1 duckling, boned, the meat cut into slices
2 tbsps Chinese wine
1 tbsp soy sauce
1 tbsp hoisin sauce
1¼ cups chicken stock
Salt and freshly ground black pepper

Heat the oil in a wok and stir-fry the onions until lightly browned. Ease the onions up the side of the wok out of the oil, to keep them warm. Add the duckling to the wok and stir-fry until lightly browned. Pour in the Chinese wine. Push the onions back into the bottom of the wok, with the duckling. Stir in the soy sauce, hoisin sauce and the stock. Continue to cook until slightly reduced, then season with salt and pepper and serve immediately.

AROMATIC AND CRISPY DUCK

I once overheard a customer in a Chinese restaurant trying to sort out the differences between all the varieties of crispy duck! This one is steamed before frying, which makes the meat very tender. It is aromatic because it is rubbed with sauces and spices.

Serves 4

INGREDIENTS

1 duck, weighing 3½ pounds
2 tbsps black bean sauce
2 tbsps dark soy sauce
2 tsps five-spice powder
3 slices fresh root ginger
Oil for deep-frying
Mandarin Pancakes, (see recipe for Peking Duck)
Duck Sauce, (see recipe for Peking Duck)
½ cucumber, shredded
4 scallions, shredded

Rub the duck inside and out with the black bean sauce, soy sauce, five-spice powder and ginger. Leave in a cool place overnight.

Place the duck in a steamer and steam well for 1½ hours, then drain and dry the duck. Heat some oil for deep-frying in a wok or large saucepan. Deep-fry the duck for 10-12 minutes until very crispy. Scrape the duck meat off the bones. Roll up in the pancakes with the duck sauce, shredded cucumber and scallions.

DUCK WITH BAMBOO SHOOTS

Bamboo shoots require a great deal of preparation when they are fresh. The canned shoots loose a little of the crispy texture of the fresh vegetable but are very convenient to use. They provide more texture than flavor and help to make a little meat go a long way!

Serves 4

INGREDIENTS
1 cup bamboo shoots, cut into
    thin slices
⅓ cup sugar
⅔ cup water
1 tsp chopped fresh root ginger
1 tbsp hoisin sauce
2 duck breasts
1 tbsp oil
Salt and freshly ground black
    pepper

If using fresh bamboo shoots, cook them in lightly salted boiling water for approximately 15 minutes. Drain thoroughly and set aside. Mix the sugar and water together in a small saucepan, stirring thoroughly. Add the ginger and the hoisin sauce. Place over gentle heat. Cook until a light syrup is formed. Brush this syrup liberally over the duck breasts.

Heat the oil in a skillet and add the duck breasts, skin-side down. Sear on each side. Remove from the oil and finish cooking in a 425°F hot oven, for approximately 15 minutes. Shortly before the duck breasts are cooked, stir-fry the bamboo shoots in the oil used to seal the duck breasts. Season with salt and pepper and serve hot with the sliced duck breasts.

DUCKLING IN
FIVE-SPICE SAUCE

The aromatic spiciness of five-spice powder, combined with the crunchy texture of water chestnuts, makes a wonderful combination with duck meat.

Serves 4

INGREDIENTS

12 canned water chestnuts
½ cup bamboo shoots
1 tbsp sesame oil
1 tsp chopped fresh root ginger
1 duckling, boned, the meat cut into thin slices
4 Chinese dried mushrooms, soaked in warm water for 15 minutes, drained and chopped
1¼ cups duck stock
1 tsp five-spice powder
Salt and freshly ground black pepper
1 tsp cornstarch, combined with a little water

Rinse the water chestnuts and blanch in lightly salted boiling water for 10 minutes. Lift out with a slotted spoon and set them aside to drain. Blanch the bamboo shoots in the same water, rinse and then drain. When they are well drained, cut them into thin matchsticks.

Heat the sesame oil in a wok and stir-fry the ginger and the duckling slices. Remove the ginger and duckling with a slotted spoon. Stir-fry the bamboo shoots, chopped Chinese mushrooms and water chestnuts. Pour off any excess fat from the wok and return the duckling and the ginger to the wok with the vegetables. Add the duck stock and stir well. Sprinkle with the five-spice powder and cook for approximately 15 minutes. Check the seasoning, adding salt and pepper as necessary. Thicken the sauce by stirring in the cornstarch paste, stirring continuously until boiling and thickened. Serve hot.

LACQUERED DUCK

A honey and soy sauce glaze or marinade gives a rich, deep color and gloss to this dish – it is easy to see where the title "lacquered" comes from.

Serves 4

INGREDIENTS
½ tsp soy sauce
1 tbsp honey
1 tsp five-spice powder
1 tsp wine vinegar
2 cloves garlic, finely chopped
1 tsp cornstarch, combined with
   a little water
2 duck breasts
Salt and freshly ground black
   pepper

To make the marinade, mix together the soy sauce and the honey, add the five-spice powder and stir well. Stir in the vinegar, garlic and cornstarch. Season the breasts with a little salt and pepper and place in a baking dish. Pour the marinade over so that it coats the duck breasts completely. Leave to marinate for 24 hours.

Cook the duck for approximately 20 minutesin a 425°F oven, basting frequently with the marinade. To caramelize the tops, place under a hot broiler for several minutes until crispy. Watch carefully to make sure the duck breasts do not burn.

DUCK WITH
GINGER SAUCE

This is a good way of using up duck legs. People always ask for the breast but there is quite a lot of meat on the legs! The slight citrus flavor of the fresh ginger complements the duck well.

Serves 4

INGREDIENTS
4 duck legs
10 slices fresh root ginger, peeled
2 tbsps oil
1 scallion, chopped
2 cloves garlic, finely chopped
1 tbsp soy sauce
1¼ cups duck stock
1 tsp cornstarch, combined with
    a little water
Salt and freshly ground black
    pepper

Chop off the ends of the duck legs and discard. Using a small sharp knife, slide the blade down the sides of the thigh bone and ease away all the meat. Cut the meat into large slices. Cut the slices of ginger into fine strips

and place a little ginger on each slice of meat, then roll up and tie securely with thin kitchen string.

Heat the oil in a wok and stir-fry the scallions with the garlic. Add the duck rolls, together with any leftover duck meat, and fry for 2 minutes. Pour off any excess fat from the wok. Stir in the soy sauce, any leftover ginger and the stock. Simmer for about 20 minutes, until the duck has cooked through completely. Thicken the sauce with the cornstarch paste if necessary. Check the seasoning, adding salt and pepper as required. Cut the string from each duck roll and serve hot, with the sauce.

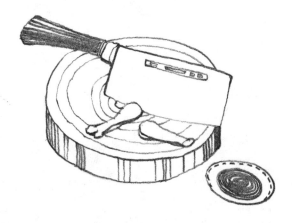

DUCKLING SALAD WITH SWEET & SOUR SAUCE

This is a simple but delicious salad. Garnish with carved vegetables if you are artistic and creative! This salad could be served as an appetizer, in which case it would serve 4 people.

Serves 2

INGREDIENTS

1 cooked duckling, cooled and
boned
½ cucumber
2 carrots
2 tbsps white wine vinegar
1 tsp mustard
1 tsp sugar
1 tbsp soy sauce
¼ cup hoisin sauce
1 tsp sesame oil
1 tbsp peanut oil
Salt and freshly ground black
pepper

Cut the duckling meat into bite-size chunks, cut the cucumber into thin slices, and the carrots into thin strips. Beat the vinegar, mustard and sugar together in a small bowl. Add the soy sauce, followed by the hoisin sauce. Lastly, beat in the sesame and peanut oils. Season with salt and pepper to taste.

Divide the duckling meat and the vegetables evenly between individual plates. Pour a little of the sauce over each portion and serve.

DUCK WITH MANGOES

The beautiful, aromatic flavor of the mangoes helps to counteract any excess fattiness in the duck and provides a perfect blend of ingredients. Mangoes will be heavily perfumed when they are ripe for eating.

Serves 4

INGREDIENTS
2 ripe mangoes
1¼ cups duck stock
2 duck breasts
3 cloves garlic, finely chopped
1 tsp finely chopped fresh root ginger
Salt and freshly ground black pepper
2 tbsps oil
1 tsp vinegar
1 tbsp freshly chopped chives

Peel the mangoes. Using a sharp knife, remove the two cheeks of fruit from each mango, then cut them into slices. Blend the slices from half a mango with the stock in a blender or food processor until smooth.

Rub the duck breasts with the garlic and ginger and season with salt and pepper. Heat the oil in a skillet or wok and seal the duck breasts all over. Remove the duck breasts and finish cooking on a baking sheet in a 425°F oven for 15-20 minutes.

Reduce the mango stock mixture by half by boiling it rapidly with the vinegar in a small saucepan, adding salt and pepper to taste. Heat the remaining mango slices in a steamer for 1 minute. Slice the duck breasts and serve them with the hot mango slices, topped with the sauce. Sprinkle with the chives just before serving.

DEEP-FRIED
BONELESS DUCK

Another variation on crispy spiced duck! In this recipe the duck is simmered in a spiced stock before being fried. Take the cooked duck meat from the bones in large pieces before frying.

Serves 4

INGREDIENTS

1 duck weighing 3½ pounds
1 egg, lightly beaten
¼ cup cornstarch
2 tbsps all-purpose flour
⅔ cup soy sauce
1½ cups beef stock
4 cloves garlic
3 tsps five-spice powder
3-4 pieces star anise
Oil for deep-frying
1 crispy lettuce, separated into leaves
½ quantity Duck Sauce (see recipe for Peking Duck)

Simmer the whole duck in a large pan of boiling water for 4-5 minutes, then drain the duck on a rack. Mix the egg, cornstarch and flour to a smooth batter.

Mix the soy sauce, stock, garlic and five-spice powder together, then simmer with the star anise for 3-4 minutes in a large pan. Add the duck, and coat well with the sauce. Simmer for 40 minutes, turning the bird over every 10 minutes. Remove the duck from the pan and drain thoroughly. Remove the meat from the bones of the duck and coat it in the batter mixture.

Heat the oil for deep-frying in a wok or saucepan. Deep-fry the duck meat for 3-4 minutes, until very crispy. Cut into 2-inch pieces. Arrange the meat on a serving platter. Eat, wrapped in crispy lettuce leaves, with the Duck Sauce.

PORK, BEEF & LAMB

To the vast majority of Chinese meat is pork!

Meat is Pork!

Pigs are farmed throughout China, especially in the south, in the Canton region. In the late 1980s there were about 335 million pigs in China, representing more than 40 per cent of the world's total pig population. It will therefore come as very little surprise that pork is the most widely eaten meat in the country!

As in all Chinese cuisine, the cooking time for meat dishes is very short. Most meat is cooked off the bone and ground, shredded or very finely sliced. Of course, the better cuts are particularly suitable for cooking in this way and many

of the pork recipes in this chapter require lean, comparatively expensive cuts such as tenderloin. This does not mean that Chinese cooking is expensive as very little meat is used in each dish, and it is made to go further by the addition of vegetables.

Some recipes call for joints of meat and a long slow cooking time; Shanghai Long-cooked Knuckle of Pork is one such dish. It requires an economical cut of pork, which is simmered for 2 hours, producing a meltingly tender result.

Beef, the Perfect Partner for Strong Flavors

Beef is the second most widely used meat in China and is often associated with strong seasonings and spicy sauces. Beef is eaten throughout China and is frequently cooked in oyster sauce (one of my favorite dishes). I find the marriage of beef with the sauce to be one of the most successful and simplest ways of producing a really savory and tasty meal.

As with pork, it is the leanest and most luxurious cuts of beef that are most frequently used for Chinese cooking, but a little goes a long way and only small quantities of meat will be required for each recipe.

Lamb, a Relatively Rare Treat

Lamb is eaten far less frequently than pork or beef, and also more rarely than fish or shellfish. It is seldom found on Chinese restaurant menus in the West, so the delicious lamb recipes that are included in this chapter will probably be as much of a surprise to you as they were to me when I first read about them. Stir-fried Lamb with Sesame Seeds is lightly caramelized before the sesame seeds are sprinkled over the lamb, and there is also a delicious recipe for lamb's kidneys with asparagus.

It is surprising that there are actually more sheep than cattle in China! I haven't yet found out what happens to the ones that are not eaten! Perhaps there are more recipes for beef than for lamb because the animals are larger?

Goats, Game and other Meats

Goats are raised in many country areas by nomadic herdsmen and there are many classic recipes for goat meat. However, this is not as popular as lamb in the cities and major centers of population, and many good goat recipes have been amended and adapted to use lamb, which is less strong in flavor and more tender. Deer are to be found in the far north of the country and there are also a few in the south, so venison is also used in regional country cooking.

Meat in the Menu

The Chinese have a vast repertoire of meat dishes in their classic cuisine, and yet they are considered to be a very healthy people because they do not eat as much meat as we do in the West. What they do eat they enjoy, producing an enormous variety of dishes by combining the meat with a vast selection of vegetables and seasonings. Many dieticians would recommend that we in the West should adopt a similar style of eating.

When planning a Chinese menu for a family meal for four people it is generally recommended to serve one or two soups and four or five other dishes, at least two of which should be meat. Choose different meats if possible, perhaps one pork and one beef to balance a chicken dish, some fish and some vegetables. Choose one meat dish that is hot and spicy and one with a lighter flavor, and try to ensure that two different cooking methods are used for the dishes selected, to give variety in flavor and texture. You don't want everything to be crispy, fried and in a cornstarch thickened sauce!

PORK IN SWEET &
SOUR SAUCE

*In the most popular sweet and sour pork dish, the pork is
coated in batter and fried before it is added to the sauce.
This recipe is easier to prepare as the meat is simply stir-fried
before the sauce is added.*

Serves 4

INGREDIENTS
1 onion
¼ cucumber
½ red pepper, de-seeded
½ green pepper, de-seeded
1 slice pineapple, fresh or
　canned
¼ cup pineapple juice
3 tbsps wine vinegar
1 tsp chili sauce
1 tbsp sugar
½ tomato, skinned, de-seeded
　and crushed
1½ cups chicken stock
2 tbsps oil
1 pound pork, cut into thin strips
1 clove garlic, chopped
1 tsp cornstarch, mixed with
　1 tsp water
Salt and freshly ground black
　pepper

Cut the onion, cucumber, red
and green peppers and
pineapple into thin matchsticks.
Mix together the pineapple juice,
vinegar, chili sauce, sugar,
crushed tomato and chicken
stock.

Heat the oil in a wok, then stir-
fry the pork and the garlic. When
the meat is golden brown,
remove it with a slotted spoon
and set aside. Add all the
vegetables and the pineapple to
the wok and stir-fry for 2
minutes. Return the pork to the
wok with the vegetables and
pineapple and pour in the sauce
mixture. Cook for 3-4 minutes,
stirring, and shaking the wok
from time to time. Thicken the
sauce by adding the cornstarch
paste, and stir continuously until
boiling and thickened. Season to
taste with salt and pepper. Serve
very hot.

SZECHUAN "YU HSIANG" PORK RIBBONS, QUICK-FRIED WITH SHREDDED VEGETABLES

This dish is hot in typically Szechuan style! If you cannot get authentic Szechuan pickles use hot Indian pickles or an Indonesian pepper sambal – it's not the same, but it still makes your nose tingle!

Serves 4

INGREDIENTS
¾ pound lean pork
3 slices fresh root ginger, peeled
2 cloves garlic
¼ cup Szechuan pickles
1 cup snow peas
1 red pepper, de-seeded
2 young carrots
2 dried chilies
¼ cup oil
1 cup shredded white cabbage
½ cup beansprouts
1 tsp salt
¼ cup stock
3 tsps sesame oil

Sauce
3 tbsps soy sauce
2 tbsps Hoisin sauce
1 tbsp chili sauce
2 tbsps vinegar

Cut the pork into very thin slices, then cut it again into 1-inch strips. Cut the ginger, garlic, pickles, snow peas, pepper, carrots and chilies into small slices. Mix together the ingredients for the sauce.

Heat the oil in a wok. When hot, add the chilies, pickles, pork and ginger. Stir over high heat for 2 minutes. Add all the shredded vegetables and the beansprouts. Sprinkle with salt, and stir over the heat for 2 minutes. Add the stock and cook for a further 2 minutes. Add the sauce ingredients and sesame oil, and continue stir-frying for a further 2 minutes. Serve on a well-heated platter with steamed rice.

STIR-FRIED SLICED PORK WITH PIGS' LIVER AND KIDNEY

This recipe makes good use of both pigs' liver and kidney, mixing them with lean pork meat, snow peas and water chestnuts.

Serves 4

INGREDIENTS
1 pig's kidney
¼ pound lean pork loin
¼ pound pigs' liver
1 cup snow peas
6 water chestnuts
⅓ cup oil
1 scallion, finely sliced

Marinade
1½ tbsps white wine
1½ tbsps soy sauce
1½ tbsps cornstarch
1 tsp sugar

Sauce
½ tsp freshly ground black pepper
½ tsp vinegar
1 tsp cornstarch
½ tsp salt
½ tsp sugar
½ tsp sesame oil
2 tbsps water

Soak the kidney in cold water for 30 minutes, then skin it and remove the core. Cut the pork, liver and kidney into thin slices. Prepare the marinade for the meats by mixing all the ingredients together. Divide between three separate bowls and marinate the pork, liver and kidney separately for 30 minutes. Shred the snow peas and slice the water chestnuts.

Mix the ingredients for the sauce together, and set aside. Set a wok over high heat for 30 seconds and pour in ¼ cup of the oil. Heat until almost smoking, then lower the heat slightly and stir in the pork, liver and kidney. Stir-fry for 2-3 minutes, then remove the meats with a slotted spoon. Add the remaining oil to the wok. Stir-fry the snow peas and water chestnuts for 1-2 minutes, then add the sauce mixture. If the mixture becomes too thick, add more water. Cook until a thick, transparent paste is formed, then stir in the pork, liver and kidney. Add the scallion and place on a warmed serving dish. Serve immediately.

MEAT BALLS WITH BAMBOO SHOOTS

Chopped chives bring freshness to this dish. Do not chop them until just before using, or they will lose much of their flavor. Dried chives are simply not the same!

Serves 4

INGREDIENTS

½ pound boneless chicken
½ pound lean pork
1 clove garlic, chopped
1 tbsp freshly chopped chives
1 egg, lightly beaten
Salt and freshly ground black
  pepper
1¾ cups bamboo shoots
2 tbsps oil
1 scallion, chopped
½ tsp chopped fresh root ginger
¾ cup chicken stock
1 tsp cornstarch, combined with
  a little water

Grind the chicken and pork in a food processor or grinder with half of the garlic and chives. Place the meat in a bowl and add the egg. Beat well with a fork, and season with salt and pepper. Cut the bamboo shoots into thin, even slices and blanch in boiling, salted water. Rinse under cold water and drain.

Heat 1 tbsp of the oil in a skillet or wok. Shape the meat in your hands to form small, flat circles and fry on both sides until almost cooked. Heat the remaining oil in a separate wok and stir-fry the scallion, remaining garlic and chives, and the ginger and bamboo shoots for 2 minutes. Stir in the chicken stock and cook to reduce. Season again with salt and pepper and add the cornstarch paste. Stirring continuously until the sauce boils and thickens. Cut the meat circles into even-size strips and finish cooking them in a Chinese steamer. Serve the meat with the bamboo shoots and sauce.

STEAMED PORK WITH GROUND RICE

This spiced pork is dredged in ground rice, which makes a deliciously grainy-textured coating. The steaming makes the meat moist and tender. Szechuan chili bean paste is available in specialist food shops and Chinese supermarkets.

Serves 4-6

INGREDIENTS
1½ pounds pork tenderloin
1 tsp salt
2 tbsps soy sauce
2 tbsps Szechuan chili bean paste
1 tsp sugar
3 slices fresh root ginger, peeled and finely shredded
3 shallots, finely chopped
Freshly ground Szechuan pepper
1 tbsp oil
¼ cup ground rice
1 head Bok Choy, shredded

GARNISH
Sesame oil
3 scallions, finely chopped

Cut the pork into bite-size pieces. Mix together the salt, soy sauce, chili bean paste, sugar, ginger, shallots, Szechuan pepper and oil. Add the prepared pork and marinate for 20 minutes.

Coat each piece of pork with ground rice. Arrange in neat layers on a bed of the shredded Bok Choy in a steamer. Steam well for 25-30 minutes.

Serve the pork on a bed of the shredded Bok Choy. Garnish with sesame oil and scallions. Serve with a chili sauce as a dip if wished.

SHANGHAI LONG-COOKED KNUCKLE OF PORK

Pork knuckles can be bought at bargain prices so it is good to have a few recipes to make the most of them! The meat will be well cooked after two hours and you should be able to pull it off the bone with a spoon and fork.

Serves 4-6

INGREDIENTS
3-4 pounds pork hock or
   knuckle
7½ cups water
3 shallots
⅔ cup soy sauce
¼ cup sugar
⅔ cup pale dry sherry
4 slices fresh root ginger, peeled
2 tbsps lard

Clean and trim the pork, then slash the meat with a knife so that it cooks quickly. Place in a large, deep pan and cover with the water. Bring to a boil, then simmer for 15 minutes. Discard one-third of the water.

Cut the shallots into 1-inch pieces and add them to the pork with the soy sauce, sugar, sherry, ginger and lard. Cover and simmer for 2 hours. Turn the pork over several times during cooking. By the end of the cooking time the water in the pan should have reduced by three-quarters. Return to a boil and reduce again by half. The broth or sauce will have become rich and brown.

Place the pork in a deep bowl and pour the sauce over it. Serve with steamed vegetables and rice.

PORK WITH SCRAMBLED EGGS

A very high protein dish to be served with noodles and stir-fried, crispy vegetables.

Serves 4

INGREDIENTS
8 eggs
½ onion, finely chopped
1 tbsp oyster sauce
Salt and freshly ground black
　pepper
1 pound lean pork
2 tbsps oil
1-2 cloves garlic, chopped
3-4 small Chinese dried black
　mushrooms, soaked for 15
　minutes in warm water
1 tsp sugar
½ tsp soy sauce
1 cup chicken stock
1 tsp cornstarch, combined with
　a little water

Beat the eggs together with the onion, oyster sauce and a little pepper. Set aside. Cut the meat into very thin slices. Rinse and drain the mushrooms.

Cook the eggs over very gentle heat in a skillet, stirring constantly with a wooden spoon or a spatula until thickened. This should take approximately 10 minutes. Meanwhile, heat the oil in a wok and stir-fry the garlic and the pork. Pour off any excess fat and add the mushrooms, sugar, soy sauce and the stock. Cook until the meat is cooked through. Thicken with the cornstarch paste, stirring continuously until the sauce boils and thickens. Place a bed of scrambled eggs on a warm plate and arrange the meat mixture over the eggs.

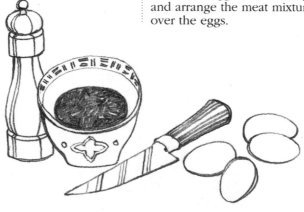

PORK WITH CHINESE VEGETABLES

Add a few fresh mushrooms toward the end of cooking if you like. The sauce for this marinated pork is flavored with garlic and ginger.

Serves 4

INGREDIENTS

1 pound pork tenderloin
1-2 cloves garlic, chopped
½ tsp chopped fresh root ginger
½ tsp cornstarch
¼ tsp chili sauce
1 tbsp wine vinegar
1 tbsp soy sauce
1 cup bamboo shoots
6-8 Chinese dried black
   mushrooms, soaked for 15
   minutes in warm water
2 tbsps oil
1¼ cups chicken stock

Cut the pork into small dice. Add the garlic and ginger, and sprinkle with the cornstarch. Add a little chili sauce – not too much as it is very hot – then the vinegar. Finally sprinkle with the soy sauce. Leave to marinate for 20 minutes at room temperature.

Cut the bamboo shoots into thin strips. Blanch them in boiling, lightly salted water, then rinse in cold water and set aside to drain. Rinse the mushrooms and set aside to drain. Remove the meat from the marinade with a slotted spoon and reserve the marinade.

Heat the oil in a wok and stir-fry the meat until tender. Pour off any excess fat and pour in the stock. Stir in first the mushrooms and the bamboo shoots and then the marinade. Cook together until boiling and thickened. Serve hot.

STUFFED BOK CHOY

Serve these stuffed Bok Choy leaves on a bed of special fried rice. Make certain that the leaves are soft before you fill them, or they will tear instead of rolling up neatly.

Serves 4

INGREDIENTS
½ pound lean pork
½ pound boneless chicken
½ pound Bok Choy
1 tbsp oil
1-2 cloves garlic, chopped
½ cup beansprouts, blanched
2 tbsps sweetcorn
2 tbsps soy sauce
Salt and freshly ground black
  pepper
2 cups duck stock
1 tsp cornstarch, combined with
  a little water
Soy sauce to taste

Chop the pork and the chicken finely. Reserve 8 Bok Choy leaves and shred the remaining leaves finely. Blanch the reserved leaves in boiling water until soft, then refresh them in cold water and dry on a dish cloth.

Heat the oil and stir-fry the meat, garlic, shredded Bok choy leaves, beansprouts, sweetcorn, 1 tbsp of the soy sauce, salt and pepper for several minutes. Spread the blanched leaves out and place a small amount of stuffing on each one. Roll up each leaf around the stuffing, beginning at the base and folding in the sides halfway up, to enclose the filling completely. Secure the rolls with wooden cocktail sticks if necessary.

Heat together the stock and the remaining soy sauce. Drop the stuffed rolls into the stock and cook for 5 minutes, turning occasionally. Remove the rolls with a slotted spoon and place them on a heated serving plate. Thicken the sauce by adding the cornstarch paste. Heat, stirring continuously, until boiling and thickened. Adjust the seasoning as necessary. To serve, surround the rolls with the sauce, flavored with a few drops of soy sauce.

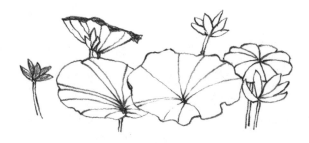

PORK WITH BAMBOO SHOOTS

Zucchini and bamboo shoots provide contrasting textures to accompany thin slices of pork. Any left-over zucchini may be added to a vegetable stir-fry.

Serves 4

INGREDIENTS
1 pound lean pork
Salt and freshly ground black pepper
1 cup bamboo shoots
1 zucchini
2 tbsps oil
1 scallion, chopped
½ cup chicken stock
1 tbsp soy sauce
1 tsp cornstarch, combined with a little water

Cut the pork into very thin slices and season with salt and pepper. Cut the bamboo shoots into small squares and blanch in lightly salted boiling water for 2 minutes. Drain well. Using a sharp knife, peel the zucchini thickly lengthwise. Discard the remaining flesh and seeds. Slice the peel thinly into strips.

Heat the oil in a wok. Add the scallion and the meat. Stir-fry for 1 minute. Pour off any excess fat and stir in the stock. Add the bamboo shoots and the zucchini and cook gently for 6-8 minutes. Stir in the soy sauce and add the cornstarch mixture, stirring continuously until the sauce has boiled and thickened. Add salt and pepper to taste. Serve hot.

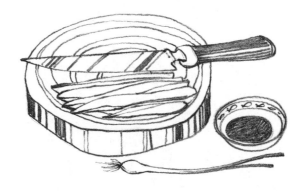

CARAMELIZED PORK

Pork tenderloin cooks quickly. I would serve this with egg noodles, stir-fried mushrooms and Bok Choy.

Serves 4

INGREDIENTS
2 tbsps dark soy sauce
1 tbsp Chinese wine
1 tbsp hoisin sauce
1 tsp honey
¼ tsp chili sauce
2 tsps oil
1 pound pork tenderloin
Salt and freshly ground black
  pepper

Mix together the soy sauce, wine, hoisin sauce, honey, chili sauce and oil. Stir well. Cut any excess fat from the pork tenderloin and remove any gristle. Tie the meat up with thin kitchen string to make a neat shape. Place the meat in a baking dish. Coat with the prepared sauce and cook in a 350°F oven for 30 minutes. Baste the pork with the sauce during cooking, so that it builds up in caramelized layers around the meat. Remove the pork from the oven and place it on a carving board. Pour any remaining sauce into a sauce boat.

Cut the meat into paper thin slices and arrange on a warmed serving dish. Serve immediately with any remaining sauce.

PORK SPARERIBS WITH CHINESE MUSHROOMS

The sauce for these spareribs is slightly hotter than some as it contains chili sauce. Add as much as you like.

Serves 4

INGREDIENTS
2 pounds pork spareribs
1 carrot, finely sliced
1 leek, finely chopped
1 bay leaf
3 cups Chinese dried mushrooms, soaked for 15 minutes in warm water and drained
1 tbsp oil
2-3 cloves garlic, chopped
½ tsp chili sauce
1 tbsp soy sauce
1 tbsp hoisin sauce
1 tsp wine vinegar
1¼ cups chicken stock
Salt and freshly ground black pepper

Chop the spareribs into small pieces. Boil plenty of water with the carrot, leek and bay leaf in a large pan. Blanch the spareribs for 1 minute in the boiling water, then drain them well. Cook the mushrooms in the boiling water for 10 minutes, then drain them well too.

Heat the oil in a wok. Add the garlic, chili sauce and mushrooms. Fry slowly until lightly colored, then stir in the soy sauce, hoisin sauce, vinegar and stock. Add the spareribs, stirring so that they are well coated with the sauce. Season with salt and pepper to taste. Cook, covered, for 10 minutes. Remove the lid and allow the sauce to reduce slightly. Serve very hot.

PORK WITH GREEN PEPPERS

This simple stir-fry celebrates the fresh flavor of green peppers. The only other vegetables included are for seasoning purposes, so the green peppers really dominate the dish.

Serves 4

INGREDIENTS
1 pound pork tenderloin
2 tbsps oil
1-2 cloves garlic, chopped
2 green peppers, de-seeded and cut into thin matchsticks
1 tsp wine vinegar
2 tbsps chicken stock
1 tbsp hoisin sauce
Salt and freshly ground black pepper
1 tsp cornstarch, combined with a little water

Slice the pork thinly, then cut it into narrow strips. Heat the oil in a wok. Add the garlic, green peppers and the meat. Stir well and cook for 1 minute, shaking the wok occasionally. Stir in the vinegar, stock and hoisin sauce. Season to taste with salt and pepper and cook for a further 3 minutes. Stir in the cornstarch and cook, stirring continuously, until boiling and thickened. Serve at once.

STIR-FRIED PORK AND VEGETABLES

Shaohsing wine is rice wine – dry sherry may be used if preferred. The sauce for this pork dish is spicy and very slightly sweet.

Serves 4

INGREDIENTS

1 carrot, cut into thin matchsticks
1 cup beansprouts
2 tbsps oil
1 slice fresh root ginger
1 scallion, chopped
1-2 cloves garlic, chopped
1 pound pork, cut into thin slices
2 tsps Shaohsing wine
1¼ cups chicken stock
Salt and freshly ground black
 pepper
½ tsp brown sugar
1 tsp cornstarch, combined with
 a little water

Boil a little salted water in a small saucepan. Blanch the carrot strips for 1 minute. Drain well, reserving the water. Wash the beansprouts under running water then blanch them for 1 minute in the water, used for the carrot. Rinse well and drain.

Heat the oil in a wok. Stir-fry the ginger, scallion and garlic until slightly colored, then add the meat. Stir well and cook for 1 minute. Add the well-drained vegetables, wine and stock. Season with salt and pepper, and stir-fry for 2 minutes. Using a slotted spoon, remove the meat and vegetables, and keep warm. Add the sugar to the contents of the wok and thicken the sauce with the cornstarch paste, stirring until boiling and thickened. Remove the ginger, return the meat and vegetables to the wok and serve hot.

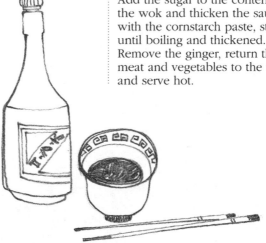

LION'S HEAD

This recipe title describes the meat balls sitting on a "mane" of cabbage! Use Chinese cabbage, or Bok Choy, but do not shred the leaves or they will overcook. Serve as part of a mixed buffet meal.

Serves 6

INGREDIENTS

2 pounds ground pork
2 shallots, finely chopped
2 slices fresh root ginger, peeled and finely chopped
2 tbsps pale dry sherry
2 tbsps cornstarch
1 tsp salt
2 tbsps lard
1 pound Chinese cabbage or Bok Choy, quartered lengthwise
1¼ cups chicken stock

Mix together the pork, shallots, ginger, sherry, cornstarch, and half the salt. Shape the mixture into six meat balls. Melt the lard in a deep pan. Add the cabbage and remaining salt, and fry for 30 seconds. Place the meat balls on the cabbage and pour the stock over the top. Bring to a boil, then cover the pan tightly. Simmer gently for 30-40 minutes. Serve hot. (Alternatively the meat balls may be fried in a little lard, with soy sauce and sugar, before placing them on top of the cabbage.)

PORK SLICES WITH CRUNCHY VEGETABLES

This is a very light, summery dish: steamed pork with crispy steamed vegetables served with a fragrant, cold sauce.

Serves 4

INGREDIENTS
1 tbsp light soy sauce
1 tbsp Chinese wine
1 tsp sugar
1-inch piece of fresh root ginger, peeled and finely chopped
1 pound lean pork
Salt and freshly ground black pepper
1 carrot
1 stick celery
½ fennel

To make the sauce, mix together the soy sauce, Chinese wine, sugar and ginger in a small bowl. Let stand for 30 minutes for the flavors to blend before serving.

Cut the pork into very thin slices and season with salt and pepper. Cut the carrot, celery and fennel into thin strips. Place the vegetables in a steaming basket and steam for 3 minutes. Remove the basket from the steamer and lay the slices of pork over the vegetables. Return the basket to the steamer and cook for another 5 minutes. Serve the steamed pork and vegetables accompanied by the cold sauce.

BRAISED PORK WITH SPINACH & MUSHROOMS

Spinach and nutmeg are used together in many international cuisines. You might think that such delicate flavors would get lost in this dish, but not at all – try it and see.

Serves 4

INGREDIENTS

4 Chinese dried mushrooms
2 tbsps peanut oil
½ tsp ground nutmeg
½ pound spinach leaves, washed, stalks removed, and shredded
1 clove garlic, crushed
1 onion, quartered
1 tbsp flour
Salt and freshly ground black pepper
1 pound pork tenderloin, cut into thin strips
2 tbsps water

Soak the mushrooms in hot water for 20 minutes, then drain. Discard the stems, slice the caps finely and set aside. Heat a wok, add 1 tsp of the oil and roll it around to coat the surface of the wok. Add the nutmeg and spinach and cook gently for 5 minutes, then remove the spinach from the pan. Add the remaining oil to the wok and fry the garlic and onion over gentle heat for 5 minutes. Remove from the wok.

Meanwhile, season the flour with salt and pepper and use it to coat the pork. Fry the pork in the wok until each piece is brown all over. Add the water and mushrooms, and return the onion mixture to the wok. Cover and simmer gently for 10 minutes, stirring occasionally. Add the spinach and season to taste, then cook, uncovered, for 2 minutes. Serve hot with steamed rice.

PORK WITH CHILI

Always take great care to remove the seeds from peppers and chilies – that's where the real heat is hidden! Slice or chop chilies very finely and rinse your hands after preparation to remove all the strong juices.

Serves 4

INGREDIENTS
1 clove garlic, crushed
1 tsp sugar
1 tsp peanut oil
1 tsp Chinese wine or dry sherry
1 tsp cornstarch
¾ pound lean pork tenderloin, cut into 1-inch slices
⅔ cup peanut oil, for deep-frying
1 green pepper, de-seeded and sliced
1 red chili, de-seeded and finely sliced
4 scallions, chopped

Sauce
1 tsp chili powder
2 tbsps dark soy sauce
1 tsp Worcestershire sauce
½ tsp five-spice powder
Pinch of salt

Mix together the garlic, sugar, 1 tsp peanut oil, wine and cornstarch, and pour the mixture over the prepared pork. Cover and leave for at least 1 hour, stirring occasionally. Meanwhile, combine the ingredients for the sauce in a bowl, mix well and set aside.

Heat the oil for deep-frying in a wok until hot. Add the pork and fry for about 10 minutes until golden brown and cooked through. Remove the pork with a slotted spoon, drain on paper towels and set aside. Carefully remove all but 1 tbsp of oil from the wok. Heat and add the green pepper, chili and scallions. Stir-fry for 2 minutes. Add the prepared sauce and fried pork. Bring to a boil, stirring continuously. Adjust the seasoning. Serve immediately with rice or noodles.

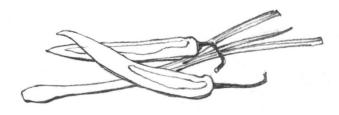

SWEET & SOUR PORK

Serves 2-4

Ingredients
½ pound pork tenderloin, cut
  into ½-inch cubes
Oil for deep-frying
1 onion, sliced
1 green pepper, de-seeded and
  sliced
8-ounce can pineapple chunks,
  juice reserved

Batter
1 cup all-purpose flour
¼ cup cornstarch
1½ tsps baking powder
Pinch of salt
1 tbsp oil
Water

Sweet & Sour Sauce
2 tbsps cornstarch
½ cup light brown sugar
Pinch of salt
½ cup cider vinegar or rice
  vinegar
1 clove garlic, crushed
1 tsp fresh root ginger, peeled
  and grated
⅓ cup ketchup
⅓ cup reserved pineapple juice

First prepare the batter. Sift the flour, cornstarch, baking powder and salt into a bowl. Make a well in the center and add the oil and enough water to make a thick, smooth batter. Using a wooden spoon, stir the ingredients, gradually incorporating the flour, and beat until smooth.

Heat enough oil in a wok to deep-fry the pork. Dip the pork cubes one at a time into the batter and drop into the hot oil – chopsticks are ideal for doing this. Fry 4-5 pieces of pork at a time and remove them with a slotted spoon and drain on paper towels. Continue frying until all the pork is cooked.

Drain most of the oil from the wok and add the sliced onion, pepper and pineapple. Cook over high heat for 1-2 minutes, then remove the vegetables and pineapple and set aside. Mix all the sauce ingredients together and pour into the wok. Bring slowly to a boil, stirring continuously until thickened. Simmer for about 1-2 minutes or until completely clear. Add the vegetables, pineapple and pork cubes to the sauce and stir to coat the pork completely. Reheat for 1-2 minutes and serve immediately.

PORK WITH BLACK BEAN SAUCE

Making your own black bean sauce for this stir-fry gives a much stronger flavor. The sauce also goes well with chicken and beef.

Serves 4

INGREDIENTS

Sauce

½ pound lean pork, cut into 1-inch cubes
1 tbsp oil
1 red pepper, de-seeded and sliced

3 tbsps black beans, rinsed in cold water and crushed with the back of a spoon
2 tbsps Chinese wine or dry sherry
1 tsp grated fresh root ginger
2 tbsps light soy sauce
3 cloves garlic, crushed
1 tbsp cornstarch
⅔ cup water

Prepare the sauce. Mix together the black beans, wine, ginger, soy sauce and garlic. Blend the cornstarch with 2 tbsps of the water and add it to the mixture. Place the pork in a bowl and cover with the sauce. Leave to marinate for at least 30 minutes.

Heat a wok, add the oil and stir-fry the red pepper strips for 3 minutes. Remove and set aside. Add the pork, reserving the marinade sauce, and stir-fry until browned all over. Add the marinade and remaining water, then bring to a boil. Lower the heat, cover the wok and simmer for about 30 minutes, until the pork is tender, stirring occasionally. Add more water during cooking if necessary. Just before serving, add the red pepper and heat through. Serve with plain boiled rice.

PORK WITH PLUM SAUCE

Plum sauce is deep red in color, spicy in flavor and a vital part of Chinese cooking. It is often served with crispy duck in pancakes. Most supermarkets sell it in bottles and you will certainly get it in specialist Chinese shops and delicatessens.

Serves 4

INGREDIENTS
1 tbsp cornstarch
1 tsp sesame oil
1 tbsp light soy sauce
1 tbsp sherry
1 tbsp brown sugar
½ tsp cinnamon
Pinch of salt
1 pound lean pork tenderloin,
  cut into 1-inch cubes
2 tbsps peanut oil
1 scallion, finely sliced
1 clove garlic, crushed
¼ cup prepared plum sauce
¼ cup water
Freshly ground black pepper
Scallion flowers (see recipe for
  Barbecued Spareribs)

Mix together the cornstarch, sesame oil, light soy sauce, sherry, brown sugar, cinnamon and salt. Pour the marinade over the pork in a bowl, toss together and leave to stand for a few minutes. Remove the pork and reserve the marinade.

Heat a wok and add the peanut oil. Add the pork, and stir-fry until golden brown all over. Stir in the scallion, garlic, plum sauce and water, and mix together well. Bring to a boil. Cover and simmer gently for 15 minutes, or until the pork is tender, stirring occasionally. Add the reserved marinade from the pork, and bring to a boil. Simmer gently for a further 5 minutes. Garnish with scallion flowers. Serve hot with boiled rice.

FIVE-SPICE BEEF WITH BROCCOLI

This is an easy recipe to prepare. The rich green of the broccoli looks wonderful against the brown of the spiced beef, garnished with long lengths of chives.

Serves 4

INGREDIENTS
½ pound beef fillet or tenderloin
1 clove garlic, crushed
½ tsp finely grated fresh root
  ginger
½ tsp five-spice powder
2 tbsps peanut oil
¼ pound broccoli flowerets
1 tbsp dark soy sauce
½ tsp salt
⅔ cup hot water
2 tsps cornstarch
1 tbsp cold water
Bunch of chives, snipped into
  1-inch lengths

Cut the beef into thin slices, then into narrow strips. Mix together with the garlic, ginger and five-spice powder.

Heat a wok, add 1 tbsp of the oil and stir-fry the broccoli for 8 minutes. Remove the broccoli and add the remaining oil to the wok. Add the beef and seasonings and stir-fry for 3 minutes. Stir in the broccoli, the soy sauce, salt and hot water, and heat to simmering point.

Blend the cornstarch and cold water. Pour into the wok and cook, stirring continuously, until boiling and thickened. Toss in the chives, stir, and serve immediately with boiled rice.

STIR-FRIED BEEF WITH OYSTER SAUCE

Stir-fried Beef with Oyster Sauce has a deep intensity of flavors with peppery overtones. Serve it with fried rice and mixed Chinese vegetables.

Serves 4

INGREDIENTS
¾ pound lean beef
⅓ pound broccoli
1¼ cups oil for deep-frying
2 tbsps oyster sauce
½ tsp salt
1 tsp sugar
2 scallions, chopped

Marinade
2 tsps white wine
1 tbsp soy sauce
½ tsp salt
1 tsp sugar
¼ tsp baking powder
¼ tsp freshly ground black pepper
1 tbsp water
2 tsps cornstarch
2 tbsps oil

Cut the beef into thin slices. Mix all the marinade ingredients together, add the beef and leave for several hours. Remove the beef with a slotted spoon and discard the marinade. Cook the broccoli, broken into flowerets, in boiling salted water for 15-20 minutes, then drain.

Heat the oil in a wok, then deep-fry the marinated beef for 20 seconds. Remove the beef with a slotted spoon. Remove all but ¼ cup oil from the wok. Stir-fry the broccoli in the remaining oil for 30 seconds. Add the beef. Sprinkle with oyster sauce, salt, sugar and chopped scallions. Stir-fry for a further 30 seconds, then serve.

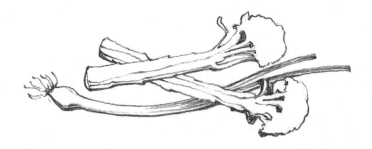

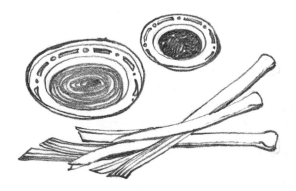

SHREDDED BEEF WITH VEGETABLES

The beef used in stir-fries cooks very quickly so it has to be of top quality to ensure that it will be tender. Fillet or tenderloin gives the best results.

Serves 4

INGREDIENTS
½ pound lean beef fillet or
  tenderloin, cut into thin strips
½ tsp salt
¼ cup vegetable oil
1 red and 1 green chili, cut in
  half, de-seeded and cut into
  strips
1 tsp vinegar
1 stick celery, cut into thin 2-inch
  strips
2 carrots, cut into thin 2-inch
  strips
1 leek, white part only, sliced
  into thin 2-inch strips
2 cloves garlic, finely chopped
1 tsp light soy sauce
1 tsp dark soy sauce
2 tsps Chinese wine or dry sherry
1 tsp superfine sugar
½ tsp freshly ground black
  pepper

Place the strips of beef in a large bowl and sprinkle with the salt. Rub the salt into the meat and leave to stand for 5 minutes. Heat 1 tbsp of the oil in a large wok. When the oil begins to smoke, lower the heat and stir in the beef and the chilies. Stir-fry for 4-5 minutes. Add the remaining oil and continue stir-frying the beef until it becomes crispy. Add the vinegar and stir until it evaporates, then add the celery, carrots, leek and garlic. Stir-fry for 2 minutes.

Mix together the soy sauces, wine or sherry, sugar and ground pepper. Pour the mixture over the beef and cook for 2 minutes. Serve immediately.

BEEF WITH ONIONS

Beef fillet is such a treat! It cooks very quickly and is always very tender. This dish uses lots of onions to flavor the meat.

Serves 4

INGREDIENTS
1 pound beef fillet
1 tbsp. oil
1-inch piece fresh root ginger,
   peeled and roughly chopped
3 onions, finely sliced
1 clove garlic, chopped
1¼ cups beef stock
Pinch of sugar
2 tbsps dark soy sauce
1 tsp cornstarch, combined with
   a little water
Salt and freshly ground black
   pepper

Marinade
1 tbsp oil
1 tsp sesame oil
1 tbsp Chinese wine

Cut the beef fillet into very thin slices. Mix together the marinade ingredients and stir in the meat. Leave for 30 minutes.

Heat 1 tbsp oil in a wok and stir-fry the ginger, onions and garlic until lightly browned. Lift the meat out of the marinade with a slotted spoon and discard the marinade. Add the meat to the wok and stir-fry with the vegetables. Add the stock, sugar and soy sauce and cook for 4 minutes. Thicken the sauce with the cornstarch mixture, stirring continuously until boiling and thickened. Season with salt and pepper and serve immediately.

MA PO TOU FU

The addition of bean curd or tofu to this recipe makes a little ground beef go a long way! The beef, even in this small amount, gives flavor and texture to the hot and spicy sauce.

Serves 4

INGREDIENTS
1 pound tofu or bean curd
2 tbsps salted black beans
3 scallions
3 cloves garlic
4 chilies, de-seeded
3 tbsps oil
¼ pound ground beef
1 tsp salt
1 cup stock
1 tbsp cornstarch
1 tbsp soy sauce
½ tsp freshly ground black
   pepper

Simmer the whole cakes of bean curd or tofu in water for 3 minutes, then drain them and cut into bite-size pieces. Soak the black beans in water for 20 minutes. Chop the scallions, garlic and chilies. Drain the black beans.

Heat the oil in a large wok. Add the beef, salt and black beans and stir-fry for 3-4 minutes. Add the chilies, scallions and garlic. Cook for a further 2 minutes before adding half the stock and the tofu. Simmer for 4 minutes.

Mix the cornstarch with the remaining stock and soy sauce. Pour the mixture into the wok, bring to a boil and simmer for 2-3 minutes. Sprinkle with the black pepper and serve with rice.

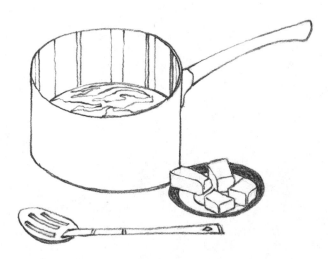

FILLET STEAK,
CHINESE-STYLE

*A little meat goes a long way in this recipe – in many
Western countries it would be quite usual for one person to
eat the amount that serves four here. Adding vegetables helps
to make the meat go further.*

Serves 4

INGREDIENTS
½ pound beef fillet or tenderloin,
   cut into 1-inch pieces
Pinch of baking soda
1 tsp light soy sauce
1 tsp sesame oil
1 tsp Chinese wine, *or* 2 tsps dry
   sherry
2 tsps sugar
1 tsp cornstarch
Salt and freshly ground black
   pepper
2 tbsps dark soy sauce
¼ cup water
3 tbsps peanut oil
2 cloves garlic, crushed
2 scallions, sliced diagonally into
   ½-inch pieces
½ tsp crushed fresh root ginger
15-ounce can straw mushrooms,
   drained
15-ounce can baby sweetcorn,
   drained
1 tbsp oyster sauce
Scallion flowers (see recipe for
   Barbecued Spareribs), to
   garnish

Place the steak in a bowl and
sprinkle with the baking soda.
Mix together the light soy sauce,
sesame oil, wine, half the sugar,
half the cornstarch, and the
seasoning. Pour over the beef
and leave for at least an hour,
turning the meat occasionally in
the marinade.

Meanwhile, make a sauce by
mixing 2 tbsps of dark soy sauce,
the remaining sugar and
cornstarch, and the water. Mix
together and set aside.

Heat a wok. Add the peanut oil
and, when hot, fry the beef for 4
minutes. Remove the beef with a
slotted spoon and set aside. Stir-
fry the garlic, scallions, ginger,
mushrooms and baby sweetcorn
briefly, then add the steak and
oyster sauce and mix well. Add
the sauce mixture and bring to a
boil. Cook for 3 minutes, stirring
occasionally. Serve hot with rice,
garnished with scallion flowers.

STIR-FRIED BEEF WITH MANGO SLICES

I have served this dish cold in buffets several times and it has always been a great success. However, it is more usual to serve it hot, with thread egg noodles or boiled rice.

Serves 4

INGREDIENTS
½ pound beef fillet
1 large mango
¼ cup oil
1 tbsp shredded fresh root ginger
1 shallot, finely sliced

Marinade
1 tbsp white wine
1 tbsp soy sauce
1 tsp cornstarch
¼ tsp sugar
¼ tsp freshly ground black pepper

Cut the beef into thin bite-size pieces. Blend together the ingredients for the marinade, add the beef and leave for 20 minutes. Peel and slice the mango.

Set a wok over high heat, add the oil and wait until almost smoking. Lower the heat to moderate, add the beef and ginger and stir-fry for 1-2 minutes. Remove the beef and ginger with a slotted spoon. Toss the mango slices in the hot oil for a few seconds, return the beef and ginger to the wok, and add the shallot. Stir-fry for a further few seconds, then serve immediately.

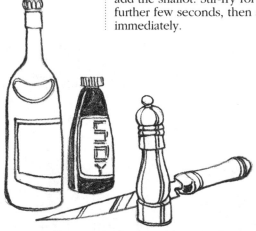

BEEF WITH TOMATO & PEPPER IN BLACK BEAN SAUCE

No extra salt is needed to season this dish as the black beans are very salty and savory. Marinate the beef in the soy sauce for at least 10 minutes.

Serves 6

INGREDIENTS
2 large tomatoes
2 tbsps salted black beans
2 tbsps water
¼ cup dark soy sauce
1 tbsp cornstarch
1 tbsp dry sherry
1 tsp sugar
1 pound beef fillet or tenderloin
1 small green pepper, de-seeded
¼ cup oil
¾ cup beef stock
Pinch of freshly ground black
 pepper

Core the tomatoes and cut them into 16 wedges. Crush the black beans, add the water and set aside. Combine the soy sauce, cornstarch, sherry and sugar in a bowl. Cut the meat into thin strips, add to the marinade and set aside. Cut the pepper into ½-inch diagonal pieces.

Heat a wok and add the oil. When hot, stir-fry the green pepper pieces for about 1 minute, then remove them with a slotted spoon. Add the meat and the soy sauce mixture to the wok and stir-fry for about 2 minutes. Add the soaked black beans and the stock. Bring to a boil. Cook until the mixture thickens slightly. Return the peppers to the wok and add the tomatoes and pepper to taste. Heat through for 1 minute and serve immediately.

BEEF WITH CHINESE MUSHROOMS

This Chinese recipe is most unusual as the meat is dry-fried, rather than being cooked in a sauce. It makes a very pleasant change.

Serves 4

INGREDIENTS

1 tsp cornstarch
1 tbsp light soy sauce
1 egg white
1 tsp sugar
1 pound beef fillet or tenderloin, thinly sliced
6 Chinese dried black mushrooms, soaked for 1 hour in warm water
2 tbsps oil
1-2 cloves garlic, chopped
Salt and freshly ground black pepper
2 tbsps Chinese wine

Place the cornstarch in a small bowl and stir in the soy sauce. Beat in the egg white and the sugar, mixing thoroughly to combine all the ingredients. Add the slices of beef and leave to marinate for 1 hour. Drain the mushrooms, which should be very soft, and cut them into thin strips.

Heat the oil in a wok. Stir-fry the garlic, the beef in its marinade and the mushrooms for 4-5 minutes and season with salt and pepper. Stir in the wine and serve as soon as it has evaporated.

SZECHUAN MEAT BALLS

Szechuan province gives its name to many classic Chinese dishes, all of which are highly spiced. Ginger, usually the fresh root variety, is one of the commonest ingredients in this vibrant style of cookery.

Serves 4

INGREDIENTS
½ cup blanched almonds
1 pound ground beef
1 tsp grated fresh root ginger
1 clove garlic, crushed
½ large green pepper, de-seeded and chopped
¼ tsp Szechuan, chili or Tabasco sauce
⅓ cup soy sauce
Oil for frying
½ cup vegetable stock
1 tbsp rice wine or white wine vinegar
2 tsps honey
1 tbsp sherry
1 tbsp cornstarch
4 scallions, sliced diagonally

Spread the almonds evenly in a pan, and broil under low heat for 3-4 minutes, or until lightly toasted. Stir the almonds often to prevent them from burning. Roughly chop the almonds using a large sharp knife, then place them in a large bowl. Add the meat, ginger, garlic, green pepper, Szechuan sauce, and 2 tbsps of the soy sauce. Using a wooden spoon, or your hands, mix well to ensure that the ingredients are well blended. Divide the mixture into 16 and roll each piece into a small meat ball on a lightly floured board.

Heat a little oil in a large skillet and add about half the meat balls in a single layer. Cook over low heat for about 20 minutes, turning the meat balls frequently until they are well browned all over. Transfer them to a serving dish and keep warm while cooking the remaining meat balls. Set aside as before.

Stir the remaining soy sauce, the stock and vinegar into the skillet and bring to a boil. Boil briskly for about 30 seconds, then add the honey and stir until dissolved. Blend the sherry and cornstarch together in a small bowl, and add the paste to the hot sauce. Cook, stirring all the time, until boiling and thickened. Arrange the meat balls on a serving dish and sprinkle with the sliced scallions. Pour the sauce over, and serve immediately.

BEEF WITH
GINGER SAUCE

Another very quick dish, both to prepare and to cook.
Chopped tomatoes give an extra richness of color to the
ginger sauce.

Serves 4

INGREDIENTS
1 pound beef fillet
2 tbsps oil
2 tbsps fresh root ginger, peeled
  and cut into small matchsticks
2 tomatoes, skinned, de-seeded
  and finely chopped
1 tsp sugar
1 tbsp red wine vinegar
2 tbsps soy sauce
Salt and freshly ground black
  pepper

Cut the beef into very thin slices. Heat the oil in a wok, add the meat and the ginger and stir-fry for 1 minute. Pour off any excess fat, and stir in the tomato. Lower the heat and add the sugar, vinegar and soy sauce. Cook for a few minutes to let the flavors develop, then season with salt and pepper to taste. Serve immediately.

BEEF WITH BLACK BEAN SAUCE

Black beans are used widely in Chinese cooking. They are soy beans which have been fermented in salt, producing a strong, savory flavor. Use them sparingly in meat and vegetable dishes. They are available canned in specialist food shops.

Serves 4

INGREDIENTS

½ pound beef fillet or tenderloin, thinly sliced
Pinch of baking soda
3 tbsps light soy sauce
3 tsps sugar
1 tsp Chinese wine *or* 2 tsps dry sherry
1 tsp sesame oil
Salt and freshly ground black pepper
¼ cup peanut oil
3 cloves garlic, crushed
1 tsp grated fresh root ginger
1 large onion, chopped
1 large green pepper, de-seeded and diced
8-ounce can bamboo shoots, drained
3 tsps black beans
1 tbsp cornstarch

Place the sliced beef in a bowl, and sprinkle it with the baking soda. Add 1 tbsp of the light soy sauce, 1 tsp of the sugar, the wine, sesame oil, salt and pepper, and leave to marinate for at least 1 hour.

Heat a wok and add 2 tbsps of the peanut oil. When hot, add the beef and the marinade and fry quickly. Remove the wok from the heat, remove the meat and juices, and set aside. Make the black bean sauce by crushing the beans and mixing with the garlic, ginger, 1 tsp of the sugar and 1 tbsp of the peanut oil.

Heat the wok, add the remaining oil and pour in the black bean mixture. Return the meat to the wok and add the onion, pepper and bamboo shoots, then mix well. Make a seasoning sauce by mixing the cornstarch with the remaining 2 tbsps of light soy sauce and 1 tsp sugar. When well mixed, pour into the wok and stir. Bring to a boil and cook for 3 minutes. Serve hot with rice.

PEKING BEEF

Cold beef, served thinly sliced after marinating or cooking in a spiced liquor, is a popular dish around the world. This version could be prepared in a heavy pan or a baking dish, but a covered wok is the traditional cooking utensil.

Serves 8

INGREDIENTS
2 pounds roast beef
2 cups white wine
2½ cups water
2 whole scallions, roots trimmed
1-inch piece fresh root ginger
3 pieces star anise
½ cup soy sauce
2 tsps sugar
1 carrot
2 sticks celery
Half a mooli (daikon) radish

Place the beef in a wok and add the white wine, water, scallions, ginger and star anise. Cover and simmer for about 1 hour. Add the soy sauce and sugar. Stir and then simmer for a further 30 minutes, or until the beef is tender. Let the beef cool in the liquid.

Shred all the remaining vegetables finely. Blanch them in boiling water for about 1 minute. Rinse under cold water, drain and leave to dry. When the meat is cold, remove it from the liquid and cut into thin slices. Arrange on a serving plate and strain the liquid over it. Scatter the shredded vegetables over the beef and serve cold.

BEEF WITH PINEAPPLE & PEPPERS

All Chinese dishes have fragrant and descriptive names. This recipe is sweet and fruity with rich and strongly contrasting flavors. Serve with plain boiled rice or noodles.

Serves 4

INGREDIENTS
2 tbsps light soy sauce
1 tsp sugar
2 tsps cornstarch
2 tbsps water
1 pound beef fillet or tenderloin, thinly sliced
1 tbsp peanut oil
1 tsp chopped fresh root ginger
2 cloves garlic, crushed
1 onion, roughly chopped
1 green pepper, de-seeded and chopped
1 red pepper, de-seeded and chopped
8-ounce can pineapple slices, drained and chopped

Sauce
1 tbsp plum sauce
1 tbsp dark soy sauce
1 tsp sugar
1 tsp sesame oil
1 tsp cornstarch
¼ cup water
Salt and freshly ground black pepper

Combine the light soy sauce with the sugar and cornstarch and 2 tbsps of water and pour over the thinly sliced beef. Toss well, then set aside for at least 30 minutes, turning occasionally.

Heat a wok and add the peanut oil. Add the ginger, garlic, onion and peppers, and stir-fry for 3 minutes. Remove the vegetables from the wok and set aside. Add extra oil if necessary and stir-fry the beef for 2 minutes, separating the pieces. Remove the beef from the wok and add it to the vegetables. Mix all the sauce ingredients together in the wok and heat until the sauce boils and begins to thicken. Return the vegetables and the beef to the wok, adding the pineapple, and toss together over high heat until heated through. Serve with boiled rice.

STIR-FRIED LAMB WITH SESAME SEEDS

Lamb is not used as widely as pork and beef in Chinese cooking. This recipe is unusual as the lightly caramelized lamb is sprinkled with sesame seeds before serving. A half lamb shoulder should be enough for the dish.

Serves 4

INGREDIENTS

1¼ pounds lamb shoulder, boned
2 tbsps oil
2 onions, thinly sliced
½ clove garlic, chopped
½ cup lamb stock or other meat stock
1 tsp sugar
1 tbsp soy sauce
½ tsp wine vinegar
Salt and freshly ground black pepper
1 tbsp sesame seeds

Cut away any excess fat from the lamb and slice the meat very thinly. Heat the oil in a wok and stir-fry the lamb. Remove when cooked and set aside. Fry the onions and garlic in the same oil until transparent, then remove them and set aside. Pour off any excess fat and put the meat back in the wok with the lamb stock, sugar, soy sauce and vinegar. Continue cooking until the sauce is reduced. Season to taste with salt and pepper. When the meat is lightly caramelized, sprinkle it with the sesame seeds and stir until the meat is evenly coated. Serve hot on a bed of the onions.

LAMB WITH
TRANSPARENT NOODLES

Transparent noodles are available in most large supermarkets and specialist food shops. They are quick to prepare and interesting to eat!

Serves 4

INGREDIENTS
1 pound lean boneless lamb
¼ pound transparent noodles
2 tbsps oil
2-3 cloves garlic, chopped
1 scallion, chopped
2 tbsps soy sauce
1 cup lamb stock
Salt and freshly ground black
 pepper

Cut the meat into thin slices. Bring a large quantity of salted water to a boil. Add the noodles and cook them for just 45 seconds. Rinse immediately in cold water and set aside to drain.

Heat the oil in a wok and stir-fry the garlic and scallion. Add the meat slices and stir-fry for 1 minute. Stir in the soy sauce and the stock and cook over gentle heat until the meat is cooked through and tender. Add the well-drained noodles and let them heat through. Adjust the seasoning, adding salt and pepper as necessary. Serve hot.

LAMBS' KIDNEYS WITH ASPARAGUS

I love kidneys and asparagus is one of my favorite vegetables, so this recipe might have been created for me! The sauce is sweet and spicy and the overall flavor of the dish is excellent.

Serves 4

INGREDIENTS
12 green asparagus spears
4 lambs' kidneys
Salt and freshly ground black
  pepper
2 cups small black Chinese dried
  mushrooms, soaked for 15
  minutes in warm water
2 tbsps oil
1 shallot, chopped
1 tsp dark soy sauce
1 tbsp hoisin sauce
1 cup chicken stock
¼ tsp chili sauce

Peel and trim the asparagus and cook in lightly salted boiling water until tender. Rinse in cold water and set aside to drain. Cut the kidneys in half, cutting out any tubes and gristle. Season with salt and pepper. Cook the mushrooms for about 10 minutes in a small quantity of boiling water. Rinse them in cold water and set aside to drain.

Heat the oil in a wok and cook the kidneys for approximately 3 minutes. Remove them and place on paper towels to remove any blood. Pour off any excess fat from the wok and add the shallot, soy sauce, hoisin sauce, mushrooms, stock and chili sauce. Cook for 2 minutes. Return the kidneys to the wok and cook until the sauce is slightly reduced. Adjust the seasoning, adding salt and pepper to taste. Reheat the asparagus by steaming lightly. Serve hot, with the kidneys in their sauce.

VEGETABLES

The tradition of vegetarian cuisine is rooted in the ancient Buddhist monasteries of China, and the influence of their wonderfully fragrant and varied cooking is clearly seen in many of the vegetable dishes that are enjoyed throughout China.

Stir-frying for Crisp, Flavorsome Results

Both steaming and cooking in a hot, sweet sauce or gravy give lightly cooked vegetables which retain a surprising degree of crispiness. However, it is the popular and most widely used method of Chinese cooking, stir-frying, that is the ideal way to produce the crispy, crunchy vegetables that are so much a part of Chinese cooking.

The advantages of stir-frying are numerous: it's quick, it retains the bright colors of the vegetables, leading to attractive presentation, and it retains many of the vitamins and minerals that are lost when vegetables are boiled. Vitamin C is found in many vegetables. It is water-soluble and therefore destroyed by boiling in water, so stir-frying is a good cooking method for vegetables.

It's Knowing When to Stop!

Well, you might say that about many of the hazards and pitfalls of life, but in this instance I am merely offering a gentle culinary suggestion that will ensure successful vegetable cooking! So many vegetable dishes are absolutely ruined because they are overcooked, leaving a lifeless mush of colorless, watery remains. I always think that the cooking of vegetables is one of the most difficult things about entertaining at home, if you want to appear relaxed and to be able to sit down with your guests. With Chinese cooking, and especially with stir-frying, it is easy to produce one or two dishes of vegetables in just a few minutes before your guests come to the table.

Very few vegetables are eaten raw in China and even salads are comprised of vegetables that have been lightly cooked. Our recipe for Bok Choy Salad with Mushrooms is a typical example of a salad served hot, with the vegetables stir-fried; whilst for the Beansprout Salad the beansprouts cooked and then chilled with the other vegetables before serving.

An Ever-changing Cuisine

No truly great traditions remain unchanged if they are to stay healthy. Chinese cooking, like that of the French, is constantly adapting its great dishes of centuries past to include new cooking techniques and foods that have recently arrived from foreign shores.

China is such a diverse and ancient civilization that it is almost impossible to believe that the Chinese haven't had everything available in some part of the country for ever! This is not so, and many vegetables – such as tomatoes and sweet potatoes – have been introduced to Chinese cooking relatively recently. When you consider the amount of carrots that are found in Chinese restaurants, and the glorious carrot sculptures that are so often centerpieces of Chinese buffets, it is almost

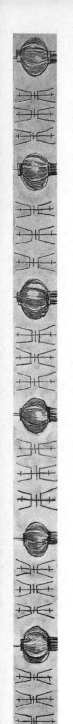

incredible to learn that carrots, too, are a relatively new introduction to the Chinese diet.

Special Vegetables for a Special Cuisine

The Chinese use many vegetables which are common to cuisines around the world, but they also have special varieties which truly make an Oriental dish. Many of these are available canned throughout the world but, of course, when at all possible, fresh is best.

Beansprouts are usually sprouted mung beans. They are crunchy in texture and should be used on the day of purchase – they never seem to keep very well, even in the refrigerator. They are generally stir-fried for a very short time, but may be cooked for longer in a dish that is served with a gravy-like sauce. Canned beansprouts are, in my opinion, the least successful of all "convenience" Oriental vegetables and are totally lacking in texture.

Bamboo Shoots are only really available fresh in the Far East. Elsewhere they are cooked and canned – I find these most acceptable, but I have never been lucky enough to get the fresh shoots. They are cut when about 6 inches high, then stripped of their outer layers and cooked. The roots are conical in shape and slices are taken from them, producing the strips of bamboo shoot with which we are all familiar.

There are several varieties of *Water Chestnuts* but the most commonly used one is a tuber which is cultivated in China, Japan and the East Indies. We find these canned in our shops and supermarkets and they retain their crunchy texture well. Water chestnuts are usually sliced before being added to Chinese dishes.

STIR-FRIED BOK CHOY

A very simple vegetable dish, yet with plenty of flavor and fire from the chili.

Serves 4

INGREDIENTS
1 pound Bok Choy
2 zucchini
2 tbsps oil
2-3 cloves garlic, chopped
1 red chili, de-seeded and finely
   chopped
1 tbsp soy sauce
Salt and freshly ground black
   pepper
¼ tsp sesame oil

Shred the Bok Choy quite finely. Prepare the zucchini, first topping and tailing them and then cutting them into matchsticks. Heat the oil in a wok, add the Bok choy and garlic, and stir-fry for 2 minutes. Add the zucchini, chili, soy sauce, salt and pepper. Continue cooking for 3 minutes. Serve hot with the sesame oil trickled on the top.

VEGETABLE CHOP SUEY

Use a good variety of vegetables, all cut into even-size pieces, for this classic dish. It is served with plenty of richly flavored sauce.

Serves 4

INGREDIENTS

1 green pepper, de-seeded
1 red pepper, de-seeded
1 carrot
½ cucumber
1 zucchini, thickly peeled, center discarded
1 onion
2 cloves garlic, sliced
2 tbsps oil
2 tsps sugar
2 tbsps soy sauce
½ cup chicken stock
Salt and freshly ground black pepper

Cut all the vegetables into thin slices. Prepare the onion by slicing it in half, then into quarters, and finally into thin, even slices. Chop the garlic very finely.

Heat the oil in a wok and stir-fry the peppers and garlic for 30 seconds. Add the onion and carrot and stir-fry for a further 30 seconds. Add the cucumber and the zucchini and cook for a further 1 minute, stirring and shaking the wok continuously. Stir in the sugar, soy sauce, chicken stock, salt and pepper. Simmer until all the ingredients are blended. Serve very hot.

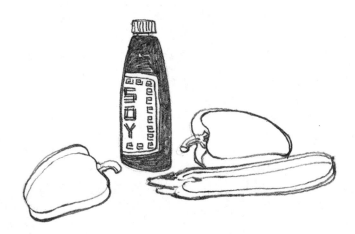

STUFFED SNOW PEAS

Stuffed snow peas are impressive as people cannot fail to notice that they are quite fiddly to prepare! Chopped mussels or shrimp could be used in place of the abalone.

Serves 4

INGREDIENTS
12 large snow peas, trimmed
1 tbsp oil
½ tsp chopped fresh root ginger
1 scallion, chopped
4 pieces abalone, diced
1 tbsp soy sauce
Salt and freshly ground black
  pepper

For the Sauce
1 tbsp vinegar
1 tsp sugar
1 tbsp soy sauce
1 tbsp freshly chopped herbs

Blanch the snow peas in lightly salted boiling water for 1-2 minutes, then set aside to drain. Slit the snow peas along one side of the pods, remove the small peas from inside and reserve.

Heat the oil in a wok and stir-fry the ginger, scallion, abalone and the small peas for 3 minutes. Stir in the soy sauce and continue cooking until the soy sauce has evaporated. Season with salt and pepper. Fill each of the snow peas with the stuffing and place them side by side in a Chinese steamer. Steam for about 4-5 minutes until completely heated through. Mix together the sauce ingredients and serve the sauce with the hot stuffed snow peas.

STEAMED ZUCCHINI FLOWERS

If you grow your own zucchini and can harvest your own zucchini flowers you may like to try this recipe. It is virtually impossible, unless you are a top chef, to buy zucchini flowers.

Serves 4

INGREDIENTS
1 pound boned pork shoulder
½ onion
1 tbsp oil
½ tsp chopped fresh root ginger
2 tbsps soy sauce
12 small zucchini with their
    flowers attached
1 drop vinegar
2 tsps sesame oil
Salt and freshly ground black
    pepper

Cut the pork shoulder and the onion into very small cubes. Heat the oil in a wok and stir-fry the ginger, pork and onion for 1 minute. Stir in ½ tsp of soy sauce and set aside.

Wash the zucchini and their flowers, then steam them for 30 seconds in a Chinese steamer. Refresh them by plunging into cold water. Open up the flowers by stretching them gently with your fingers. Stuff the meat filling inside the flowers, down between the petals. Close the flowers again by pulling the petals back into place, forming a ball at the end of each zucchini. Put the zucchini back in the steamer and cook for 4 minutes. Reheat the remaining meat stuffing in the wok. Mix together the remaining soy sauce, the vinegar and sesame oil and season with salt and pepper. Pour this sauce over the zucchini and their flowers. Serve with the reheated filling.

SPECIAL MIXED VEGETABLES

The secret of success with any stir-fry is to have all the ingredients prepared and chopped before you heat the wok. With such a quick cooking time this is very important.

Serves 4

INGREDIENTS
3 tomatoes, skinned, de-seeded and quartered
1 tbsp oil
1 clove garlic, crushed
1-inch piece fresh root ginger, peeled and sliced
4 Bok Choy leaves, shredded
1 cup thinly sliced flat mushrooms
¼ cup sliced bamboo shoots
3 sticks celery, sliced diagonally
⅓ cup baby corn, cut in half if large
1 small red pepper, de-seeded and thinly sliced
¼ cup beansprouts
2 tbsps light soy sauce
Dash of sesame oil
Salt and freshly ground black pepper

Skin the tomatoes by plunging them into boiling water for 5 seconds. Remove them with a slotted spoon and place in a bowl of cold water. This will make the skins easier to remove. Slip off the skins. Cut out the core using a small sharp knife. Cut the tomatoes in half and then in quarters. Use a teaspoon or a serrated edged knife to remove the seeds. Reserve the tomatoes – they are added to the wok last.

Heat the oil in a wok and add the ingredients in the order given, up to and including the beansprouts. Stir-fry the vegetables for about 2 minutes. Stir in the soy sauce and sesame oil and add the tomatoes. Heat through for 30 seconds, then serve immediately.

191

STIR-FRIED TARO AND CARROTS

*Taro is a relative of the yam and is very much like the eddo.
Both are available in many specialist shops and
supermarkets. Eddo, which is slightly smaller than taro, may
also be used for this recipe.*

Serves 4

INGREDIENTS
1 pound taro
1 tbsp oil
4 medium carrots, peeled and cut
   into circles
2 tsps hoisin sauce
½ cup beef stock
Salt and freshly ground black
   pepper

Peel the taro and cut it into thin
slices, then into matchsticks. Heat
the oil in a wok and stir-fry the
carrots and taro for 3 minutes,
shaking the wok frequently. Add
the hoisin sauce and the stock
and continue to cook until
slightly caramelized. Season with
salt and pepper and serve hot.
The vegetables should still be
quite crispy.

BRAISED EGGPLANT

*I love eggplant cooked any way, in any dish. Served braised,
the real flavor of this delicious vegetable is allowed to develop
and delight.*

Serves 6, or 3 as a main dish

INGREDIENTS
3 medium eggplant
⅓ cup stock
2 tbsps soy sauce
½ tsp sugar
2 tbsps pale dry sherry
2 tbsps finely chopped scallions

Cut the eggplant in half lengthwise and lay, cut side down, in a large flat baking dish. Mix the stock with the soy sauce, sugar and sherry and pour over the eggplant. Cover with a lid or foil and cook in a 375°F oven for 1 hour. Baste the eggplant once during cooking. Serve garnished with the finely chopped scallions.

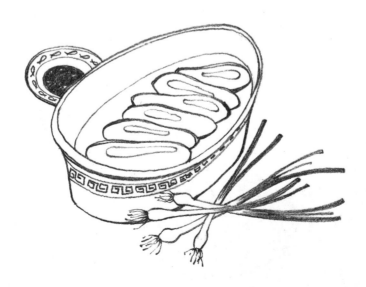

SESAME STIR-FRY

The sesame seeds give an unusual crunch to this vegetable stir-fry. Served with egg fried rice it would make an excellent supper dish for 2 people.

Serves 4

INGREDIENTS
2 tbsps vegetable oil
½ tsp grated fresh root ginger
1 tsp sesame seeds
½ cup snow peas
1 stick celery, sliced
2 baby sweetcorns, cut in half lengthwise
¼ cup thinly sliced water chestnuts
⅓ cup thinly sliced mushrooms
2 scallions, sliced diagonally
½ red pepper, de-seeded and sliced
¼ pound Bok Choy, washed and shredded
½ cup beansprouts
1 tbsp cornstarch
2 tbsps light soy sauce
1 tbsp sherry
1 tsp sesame oil
¼ cup water

Heat the oil in a wok or large skillet and fry the ginger and sesame seeds for 1 minute. Add the snow peas, celery, baby sweetcorns, water chestnuts, mushrooms, onion and pepper. Stir-fry for 5 minutes or until the vegetables are beginning to soften slightly. Add the Bok Choy and beansprouts and toss over the heat for 1 to 2 minutes. Combine the remaining ingredients in a small bowl, then add them to the pan. Continue cooking until the sauce boils and thickens slightly. Serve immediately.

QUICK-FRIED SNOW PEAS WITH BEANSPROUTS

This is a very simple dish to cook but the pickles and sesame oil flavor the vegetables well, making an unusual and exciting dish.

Serves 4

INGREDIENTS
1½ cups snow peas
1 tbsp Szechuan pickles
¼ cup oil
2 cups beansprouts
2 tsps salt
3 tbsps water
2 tsps sesame oil

Shred the snow peas finely and chop the pickles. Heat the oil in a large wok. Add the snow peas and pickles and stir-fry for 2 minutes. Add the beansprouts, salt and water and cook for a further 2 minutes. Sprinkle the vegetables with the sesame oil and serve immediately.

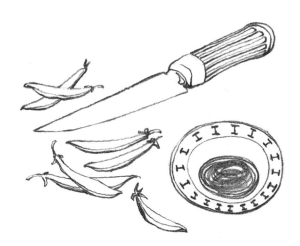

MU SHU ROU

*"Golden needles" are the dried buds of a type of lily, and
wood ears are a variety of dried mushroom. They may be
difficult to obtain if you do not have a Chinese supermarket
close by. You can use 8-10 ordinary Chinese dried
mushrooms instead, omitting the "golden needles."*

Serves 4

INGREDIENTS
2 tbsps "wood ears"
4 Chinese dried mushrooms
2 stalks "golden needles"
½ pound ground pork
3 tsps soy sauce
2 tsps water
Salt and freshly ground black
    pepper
3 scallions
2 slices fresh root ginger, peeled
3 eggs, lightly beaten
1 tsp salt
⅓ cup oil
1 tsp seasame oil
1 tsp pale dry sherry
Peking Pancakes (see recipe for
    Peking Duck) or lettuce to
    serve

Soak both types of dried
mushrooms in hot water for 15
minutes. Soak the golden needles
in hot water for 30 minutes, then
tie together, knotting in the
center to prevent them from
falling apart during cooking.
Drain and squeeze out excess
water.

Mix the pork with the soy sauce,
water, salt and pepper and leave
for 10 minutes. Drain and shred
the mushrooms, removing any
tough stalks. Drain the liquid
from the pork. Shred the
scallions and the root ginger, and
beat the eggs in a small bowl
with the salt.

Heat half the oil in a large skillet
or wok. Add the mushrooms,
golden needles and ginger and
stir-fry for 1 minute, then add the
pork and cook for a further 2
minutes. Add the scallions, stir-
fry briefly, and then remove all
the contents of the wok with a
slotted spoon.

Heat the remaining oil in the
wok, then add the beaten eggs.
Cook until just set, then return
the pork and mushroom mixture
to the wok, stirring to mix with
the egg. Sprinkle with the sesame
oil and sherry.

Serve hot, wrapped in pancakes
or crispy lettuce leaves.

TEN VARIETIES OF BEAUTY

The title of this recipe refers to the ten vegetables in it. Ten Varieties of Beauty sounds much better than Ten Vegetable Stir-fry!

Serves 4

INGREDIENTS

10 dried Shiitake mushrooms
2 carrots
¼ cup vegetable oil
3 sticks celery, trimmed and sliced diagonally
⅓ cup snow peas
8 baby corns, cut in half lengthwise
1 red pepper, de-seeded and sliced
4 scallions, sliced
¼ cup beansprouts
10 water chestnuts, sliced
¼ cup sliced bamboo shoots, drained
1¼ cups vegetable stock
2 tbsps cornstarch
3 tbsps light soy sauce
1 tsp sesame oil

Place the mushrooms in a bowl and add boiling water to cover. Leave to stand for 30 minutes, then drain and discard the stalks. Cut the carrots into ribbons using a potato peeler.

Heat the oil in a wok or large skillet and fry the celery, snow peas and baby corns for 3 minutes. Add the red pepper and carrots and stir-fry for 2 minutes, then stir in the remaining vegetables and stir-fry for 3 to 4 minutes, or until the vegetables are cooked but still crispy. Add the stock to the pan. Combine the cornstarch, soy sauce and sesame oil and stir into the pan. Cook, stirring constantly, until the sauce boils and thickens. Serve immediately.

BRAISED CELERY WITH DRIED SHRIMP & CHINESE MUSHROOM SAUCE

Braised celery is always a treat – with a Chinese Mushroom sauce and dried shrimp for extra flavor it becomes a most splendid dish.

Serves 4

INGREDIENTS
10 medium-size Chinese dried
  mushrooms
2 tbsps dried shrimp
1½ pounds celery
2 cups chicken stock
1 tsp salt
1 tbsp soy sauce
½ tsp sugar
1 tsp sesame oil
2 tsps soya oil
1½ tsps cornstarch
1 tbsp water
1 tbsp chopped scallions

Soak the Chinese mushrooms in boiling water for at least 1 hour. Soak the dried shrimp in boiling water for 30 minutes.

Drain the mushrooms and discard the hard stems. Wash and trim the celery and cut into 4-inch lengths, then place in a baking dish. Mix together ⅔ cup of the stock and the salt. Drain the dried shrimp and add them to the stock, then pour it over the celery. Cover with foil and bake in a 375°F oven for 30 minutes.

While the celery is cooking, place the mushrooms in a saucepan with the soy sauce, sugar, sesame oil, soya oil and the remaining chicken stock. Bring to a boil, then simmer for 30 minutes.

Mix the cornstarch with the water and add any cooking liquor from the celery. Add the cornstarch mixture to the mushrooms and bring to a boil, stirring all the time. Pour the thickened sauce over the celery and sprinkle with the chopped scallions before serving.

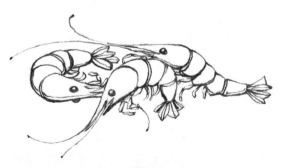

STIR-FRIED GREEN BEANS WITH CHILI

Hot and spicy green beans make an unusual and delicious Chinese-style vegetable dish.

Serves 4

INGREDIENTS
1 pound green beans
3 red chilies, de-seeded
1½ tbsps oil
1 tbsp light soy sauce
½ tsp sugar
½ tsp sesame oil

Wash and trim the beans, then cut them in half. Cook in boiling salted water for 2 minutes, then drain and rinse the beans in cold water.

Shred the chilies finely. Heat the oil in a wok and add the drained beans, chilies, soy sauce and sugar. Stir-fry for 3 minutes, then add the sesame oil. Remove the wok from the heat and serve the beans immediately.

STEAMED CABBAGE ROLLS WITH FISH AND CRABMEAT

These stuffed cabbage leaves are mildly seasoned to allow the flavor of the fish filling to develop. Serve with soy sauce and chili sauce for dipping.

Serves 4

INGREDIENTS
8 large Chinese cabbage leaves
½ pound flounder fillets, skinned
2 slices fresh root ginger, peeled
1½ tsps salt
1 egg white
1 tsp sesame oil
½ pound crabmeat
Soy sauce
Chili sauce

Pour boiling water over the cabbage leaves to soften them. Drain the leaves and dry well. Cut the fish into small pieces and finely chop the ginger. Place the fish and ginger in a bowl with the salt, egg white, sesame oil and crabmeat and mix well.

Lay the cabbage leaves out flat and divide the fish mixture between them, then roll the leaves up tightly. Secure the rolls with wooden cocktail sticks if necessary. Place the cabbage rolls in a small baking dish, then place the dish in a steamer. Steam well for 10-12 minutes.

Serve the cabbage rolls with soy sauce and chili sauce for dipping.

CANTONESE EGG FU YUNG

There are many recipes for Egg Fu Yung, which is cooked and enjoyed throughout China. Some use only egg whites but this easy recipe uses whole eggs and is served with a sauce.

Serves 2-3

INGREDIENTS

5 eggs
⅓ cup shredded cooked meat, poultry or fish
1 stick celery, finely shredded
4 Chinese dried mushrooms, soaked in boiling water for 5 minutes
¼ cup beansprouts
1 small onion, finely sliced
Salt and freshly ground black pepper
1 tsp dry sherry
¼ cup oil for frying

Sauce

1 tbsp cornstarch dissolved in 3 tbsps cold water
1¼ cups chicken stock
1 tsp ketchup
1 tbsp soy sauce
¼ tsp sesame oil

Beat the eggs lightly and add the shredded meat and celery. Squeeze all the liquid from the dried mushrooms, then discard the stems and cut the caps into thin slices. Add the mushrooms to the egg mixture with the bean sprouts and onion. Add a pinch of salt and pepper and the sherry and mix well.

Heat a wok or skillet and pour in the oil. When hot, carefully spoon in about 6 tbsps of the egg mixture. Cook until brown on one side, turn over gently and brown the other side. Remove the cooked egg to a plate and continue until all the mixture is cooked. Combine all the sauce ingredients in a small, heavy-based pan. Season with salt and pepper and bring slowly to a boil, stirring continuously until thickened and cleared. Pour the sauce over the Egg Fu Yung to serve.

EGGPLANT & PEPPERS SZECHUAN-STYLE

This hot vegetable dish could be served on its own with rice, or with a chicken or meat dish. Szechuan food is hot – you may adjust the chilies to suit your own taste!

Serves 4

INGREDIENTS

1 large eggplant
Oil for deep-frying
2 cloves garlic, crushed
1-inch piece fresh ginger, peeled and shredded
1 onion, cut into 1-inch pieces
1 small green pepper, seeded, and cut into 1-inch pieces
1 small red pepper, de-seeded and cut into 1-inch pieces
1 red or green chili, de-seeded and cut into thin strips
½ cup chicken or vegetable stock
1 tbsp sugar
1 tsp vinegar
Salt and freshly ground black pepper
1 tsp cornstarch
1 tbsp soy sauce
¼ tsp sesame oil

Cut the eggplant in half and score the cut surface with a sharp knife. Sprinkle lightly with salt and leave to drain in a colander or on paper towels for 30 minutes. Squeeze the eggplant gently to extract any bitter juices, then rinse thoroughly under cold water. Pat dry, then cut the eggplant into 1-inch cubes.

Heat about 3 tbsps oil in a wok. Add the eggplant and stir-fry for about 4-5 minutes. It may be necessary to add more oil as the eggplant cooks. Remove the eggplant from the wok and set aside.

Reheat the wok and add 2 tbsps oil. Add the garlic and ginger and stir-fry for 1 minute, then add the onion and stir-fry for 2 minutes. Add the green pepper, red pepper and chili and stir-fry for 1 minute. Return the eggplant to the wok with the remaining ingredients. Bring to a boil, stirring constantly, and cook until the sauce thickens and clears. Serve immediately.

MUSHROOM STEW

A variety of mushrooms, each with their own color and flavor, is the secret of this dish. Oyster sauce is a perfect seasoning for mushrooms.

Serves 4

INGREDIENTS

4 cups Chinese dried black
  mushrooms, soaked for 15
  minutes in warm water
4 cups Chinese dried
  mushrooms, any variety,
  soaked for 15 minutes in warm
  water
1 tbsp oil
2-3 cloves garlic, chopped
1 tbsp chopped fresh root ginger
1¼ cups chicken stock
1 tbsp oyster sauce
Salt and freshly ground black
  pepper

Cook the mushrooms in lightly
salted boiling water for 45
minutes. Rinse under cold water
and set aside to drain. Heat the
oil in a wok and stir-fry the garlic
and ginger. Add the mushrooms
and cook briefly. Add the stock,
followed by the oyster sauce and
salt and pepper to taste.
Continue cooking until the sauce
is thick and coats the
mushrooms. Serve hot.

203

STIR-FRIED TOFU SALAD

Stir-fried vegetables do not have to be eaten hot and, once cooled, they make deliciously crunchy salads. By adding tofu you are adding lots of protein, making a complete dish which requires no accompaniment.

Serves 4-6

INGREDIENTS
½ pound tofu or bean curd
1 cup snow peas
1 cup thinly sliced mushrooms
2 carrots
2 sticks celery
4 scallions
⅔ cup vegetable oil
½ cup broccoli flowerets
3 tbsps lemon juice
2 tsps honey
1 tsp grated fresh root ginger
3 tbsps soy sauce
¼ tsp sesame oil
⅓ cup unsalted roasted peanuts
½ cup beansprouts
½ head Bok Choy

Drain the tofu well and press gently to remove any excess moisture. Cut into ½-inch cubes. Trim the tops and tails from the snow peas. Slice the carrots and celery thinly, cutting at an angle to produce diagonal pieces, then trim the scallions and slice them in the same way.

Heat 2 tbsps of the vegetable oil in a wok or large skillet. Stir in the snow peas, mushrooms, celery, carrots and broccoli, and cook for 2 minutes, stirring constantly. Remove the vegetables from the wok with a slotted spoon and set them aside to cool. Place the remaining oil in a small bowl and whisk in the lemon juice, honey, ginger, soy sauce and sesame oil. Stir the sliced scallions, peanuts and beansprouts into the cooled vegetables. Mix the dressing into the vegetables, adding the tofu and tossing very carefully so that it does not break up while being mixed into the vegetables.

Shred the Bok Choy and arrange it on a serving platter. Pile the salad ingredients over the top and serve the salad well chilled.

SPINACH & RADISH SALAD

You could prepare this salad with small red radishes, although mooli would be more traditional. Use one mooli and half a bunch of red radishes for extra color.

Serves 4-6

INGREDIENTS
1 bunch radishes
Salt and freshly ground black
  pepper
2 pounds young spinach leaves
2 tbsps light soy sauce
Pinch of sugar

Clean and trim the radishes and slice them very finely, then sprinkle lightly with salt. Wash the spinach and remove any woody stems. Place in a colander and pour boiling water over the spinach to blanch it. Shake vigorously and dry on a clean dish cloth.

Place the spinach in a salad bowl and sprinkle with the soy sauce and seasonings. Add the radish and toss together before serving.

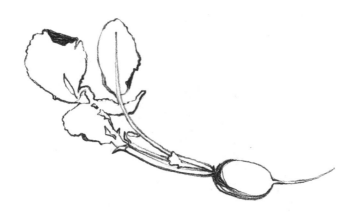

SPICED BEANSPROUTS WITH CUCUMBER SHREDS

The savoriness of the dried shrimp makes this a crunchy salad with a difference.

Serves 6

INGREDIENTS
¼ cup dried shrimp
2 pounds beansprouts
½ cucumber

Sauce
1 tbsp soy sauce
1 tsp salt
1 tbsp vinegar
1½ tsps sesame oil
1 tsp sugar

Soak the dried shrimp in boiling water for 30 minutes. Wash the beansprouts, then place them in a colander and pour boiling water over them. Drain well, then drain the shrimp. Shred the cucumber finely.

Mix all the ingredients for the sauce together. Arrange the cucumber on a platter or in the base of a salad bowl. Place the beansprouts on top, and then the dried shrimp. Pour the sauce over just before serving.

COLD TOSSED BEAN CURD

I always find tofu rather bland and tasteless but with this spicy sauce it is full of flavor. Leave it to marinate for at least 1 hour, for the tofu to become well seasoned.

Serves 4-6

INGREDIENTS
1 pound tofu or bean curd
2 tbsps chopped Szechuan
  pickles
2 tbsps dried shrimp, soaked in
  boiling water for 30 minutes
2 scallions, chopped
3 tbsps oil
1 tbsp sesame oil
2 tbsps soy sauce
Salt
1 tbsp lemon juice
3 cloves garlic, chopped
½ tsp sugar
¼ tsp freshly ground black
  pepper

Dice the bean curd into small, bite-size pieces, and place in a bowl. Sprinkle with the pickles, the soaked and well-drained shrimp and the chopped scallions.

Mix all the remaining ingredients together and pour them over the bean curd. Leave to marinate for at least 1 hour. Serve chilled.

CHINESE SALAD

Canned bamboo shoots and palm hearts may be used for this recipe if the fresh vegetables are not available – they will not be quite as crispy but they will add interesting flavors to the salad.

Serves 4

INGREDIENTS
1 head lettuce, washed and dried
4 slices ham, cut into thin strips
½ cup bamboo shoots
1 cup beansprouts, blanched in
 boiling water and drained well
1 carrot, cut into thin strips
3 palm hearts, cut in half
 lengthwise and then in half
 again
½ cucumber, cut into thin strips

Sauce
½ tsp vinegar
1 tbsp soy sauce
1 tbsp oil
1 tsp sugar
Salt and and freshly ground black
 pepper

Shred the lettuce leaves finely and mix them with the ham. Arrange on a serving plate. Prepare the bamboo shoots by slicing them first into long pieces, and then cutting the pieces in half. Blanch for 2 minutes and drain. Sprinkle the beansprouts over the lettuce and place the bamboo shoots on top. Garnish the salad with the other vegetables, making the dish look as attractive as possible. Mix the sauce ingredients together and pour them over the prepared salad just before serving.

BOK CHOY SALAD WITH MUSHROOMS

This is a warm salad of Bok Choy with a black mushroom sauce. Adding the sesame oil at the end of cooking really brings out all the flavors.

Serves 4

INGREDIENTS
12 Chinese dried black
   mushrooms, soaked for 15
   minutes in warm water
½ head Bok Choy
1 tbsp peanut oil
½ clove garlic, chopped
1 tbsp sugar
2 tbsps soy sauce
1 tbsp freshly chopped parsley
Salt and freshly ground black
   pepper
¼ tsp sesame oil

Cook the mushrooms in boiling water for 15 minutes, then set them aside to drain. Prepare the Bok Choy by separating the leaves and chopping each one into narrow strips. Blanch in boiling water for 1 minute, then refresh in cold water and leave to drain for 10 minutes.

Heat the oil in a wok and stir-fry the garlic, mushrooms and Bok Choy for 2 minutes. Stir in the sugar, soy sauce and parsley and cook for a further 2 minutes. Season with salt and pepper, trickle with the sesame oil and serve immediately.

BEANSPROUT SALAD

It may seem very Italian to use tomato sauce in a Chinese recipe. The Chinese would traditionally use crushed tomatoes – tomato sauce is much more convenient.

Serves 4

INGREDIENTS
2 cups fresh beansprouts
½ red pepper, de-seeded
1 carrot
½ cucumber
2 slices ham
1 large clove garlic, chopped
½ tsp chili sauce
2 tbsps soy sauce
Salt and freshly ground black
    pepper
1 tbsp oil
½ tsp sugar
1 drop white wine vinegar
1 tbsp tomato sauce
2 tsps sesame oil

Cook the beansprouts in boiling water for 5 minutes, then refresh them in cold water and set aside to drain and cool. Cut the pepper, carrot, cucumber and ham into thin strips. Mix the chopped garlic, chili sauce, soy sauce, salt and pepper, oil, sugar, vinegar and tomato suace together in a bowl to make a sauce. Toss the beansprouts, vegetables and ham together. Pour the sauce and the sesame oil over the vegetables and serve chilled.

COLD TOSSED BEAN CURD WITH DRIED SHRIMP

This spicy tofu salad should be served with raw mixed vegetables or cold rice. Use hot Oriental pickles if Szechuan pickles are not available.

Serves 4-6

INGREDIENTS
2 tbsps dried shrimp
2 tbsps white wine
1 pound tofu or bean curd
2 tbsps Szechuan pickles, chopped
2 tbsps chopped scallions
3 tbsps oil
2 tbsps light soy sauce
1 tbsp sesame oil
1 tbsp lemon juice
2-3 cloves garlic, crushed

Soak the shrimp in the white wine until softened, then drain and chop them finely. Chop the tofu into bite-size pieces and place in a bowl. Add the shrimp, pickles and scallions, mix well and leave for 5 minutes. Blend the remaining ingredients together and pour the sauce over the tofu. Chill before serving.

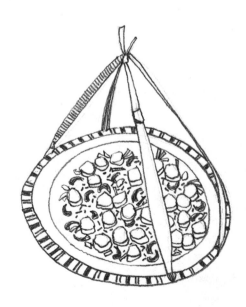

BOK CHOY AND CUCUMBER SALAD

This salad should definitely not be chilled before serving; the flavors will be reduced by the cold. I often think that salads are more flavorsome when served at room temperature.

Serves 4

INGREDIENTS
1 pound Bok Choy, sliced thinly
1 clove garlic
1 tbsp soy sauce
1 tsp sugar
2 tbsps sesame oil
¾ pound cucumber, sliced thinly
Salt and freshly ground black
   pepper

Blanch the Bok Choy in boiling, salted water for 1 minute, then set aside to drain. Prepare the garlic by first slicing the clove in half and removing the core, then crush each half with the blade of a knife and chop finely. Mix the garlic paste with the soy sauce, sugar and sesame oil. Mix the Bok Choy and the cucumber in a serving bowl and season with a little salt and pepper. Pour the marinade over the vegetables and leave at room temperature for 2 hours. Toss and serve, still at room temperature.

RICE & NOODLES

It is easy to fall into the way of thinking that rice must be served with all Chinese savory dishes as, indeed, it often is! However, there are alternatives, which include various types of noodles.

Rice – a Versatile Basic

Rice, or paddy fields, occupy almost 30 per cent of the total cultivated area of China and in the late 1980s the total annual production was around 172.4 million metric tons. It is therefore easy to see the importance of the crop to the country and to the cuisine.

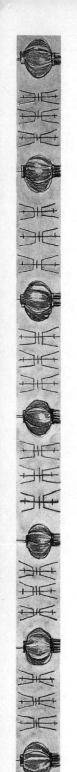

Rice is eaten throughout China, but less in the north where it is actually too cold to grow the crop successfully. Noodles and dumplings are especially popular in this area as alternatives to rice – the dumplings are more satisfying in the colder climate.

Three Varieties of Rice

The Chinese use three varieties of rice: long-grain, short-grain and glutinous rice. Purists would not contemplate the use of "easy-cook" varieties, stressing that it lacks both the color and the flavor of the long-grain rice grown in southern China. Short-grain rice is not what we in the West would call pudding rice, but a very slightly more rounded grain. It is used extensively for congee, which is traditionally served for breakfast. There are, however, many variations of congee, which include meat or poultry and are served as part of a Chinese buffet, and there are also a few sweet congees.

Glutinous rice is the most unusual rice of the three. For years we in the West have been conditioned towards separate and fluffy grains, but this is a rice that is sticky when cooked – indeed, it is often called sticky rice! It is used for both sweet and savory dishes, and is useful for stuffings. For the chopstick novice it is much easier to eat than separate grains! Glutinous rice has a high starch content which accounts for the way in which it cooks.

Boiled, "Steamed" or Fried

Boiling is the most popular international cooking method for rice but the Chinese often steam it. This does not mean that it is cooked in a container over a pan of water, but rather that it is cooked very slowly in a measured amount of water, most of which is rapidly boiled away at the start of the cooking. As a rough guide, place your rice in a pan and add water to about 1-inch above the level of the rice. Bring to a boil, then cook quickly until all the water has evaporated from the surface of the rice. Lower the heat as much as possible, then cover the pan with a tight-fitting lid and leave over low heat for about 15 minutes, resisting the temptation to peep! You should then have perfect rice.

Fried rice is the most popular rice dish in Chinese restaurants in the West. It looks interesting but, be warned! It sometimes has so many ingredients that it is more like a complete meal than an accompaniment to other dishes! There are several recipes for fried rice included in this chapter.

Chinese or Italian?

China and Italy both claim to have invented pasta and therefore noodles! Whoever made them first, both cuisines use them extensively. The Chinese use a wide variety of noodles. The most popular ones are soft, and made from wheat and egg in the same way as Italian pasta. These may be boiled and served soft, or thoroughly dried to remove any moisture after boiling and then deep-fried to achieve crispy noodles – which, I must confess, are my favorites!

Rice and Cellophane Noodles for Variety

Rice noodles are very popular in the rice growing areas of China, predominantly in the south, where they provide a welcome change from the more traditional method of cooking and serving rice. They are usually very fine and are most commonly used in soups. A type known as rice sticks is flatter and thicker, more like pasta noodles, and may be used in a variety of recipes – they make an excellent dish rather like a special fried rice when mixed with shrimp, shredded chicken and crispy vegetables.

Cellophane noodles perhaps need some explanation. They are made from a flour produced from ground mung beans and are most frequently added to savoury dishes as a filler, the complete dish then being served with rice. They are sometimes soaked to reconstitute them before being fried as a garnish.

FRIED RICE

This is a very basic recipe for egg fried rice, but one which can easily be adapted by adding cooked meat, shellfish, nuts, seeds or other vegetables. The secret is to get the rice and peas really well coated in the egg as it is just starting to set.

Serves 6-8

INGREDIENTS
3 tbsps oil
1 egg, beaten
1 tbsp soy sauce
1 pound cooked rice, well
    drained and dried
½ cup cooked peas
Salt and freshly ground black
    pepper
¼ tsp sesame oil
2 scallions, thinly sliced

Heat a wok and add the oil. Pour in the egg and soy sauce and cook until just beginning to set, then add the rice and peas and stir to coat with the egg mixture. Cook for about 3 minutes, stirring continuously. Add seasonings and sesame oil. Spoon into a serving dish and sprinkle with the scallions.

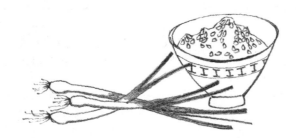

YANGCHOW SPECIAL FRIED RICE

There are so many different recipes for fried rice that I have become convinced that, for this versatile and savory dish, anything goes! It is almost a case of adding whatever is to hand.

Yangchow Special Fried Rice is one stage richer and more elaborate than ordinary fried rice. It is prepared by simply adding 1 cup cooked pork and the same amount of shrimp to basic Fried Rice (see recipe). It should not only be full of natural flavors, it should also be richly savory because of the added pork and shrimp.

SHRIMP EGG RICE

*With a simple salad garnish, Shrimp Egg Rice makes an
excellent lunch or supper dish. It is traditionally served as
part of a Chinese buffet.*

Serves 6

INGREDIENTS
2¼ cups long-grain rice
2 eggs, lightly beaten
½ tsp salt
¼ cup oil
1 large onion, chopped
1 clove garlic, crushed
⅔ cup peeled medium shrimp
½ cup shucked peas
2 scallions, chopped
2 tbsps dark soy sauce

Wash the rice thoroughly and
place it in a saucepan. Add water
to come 1 inch above the top of
the rice. Bring the rice to a boil,
stir once, then lower the heat.
Cover and simmer the rice for
5-7 minutes, or until the liquid
has been absorbed. Rinse the rice
in cold water and fluff up with a
fork, to separate the grains.

Beat the eggs with a pinch of the
salt. Heat 1 tbsp of the oil in a
wok and cook the onion until
soft, but not brown. Pour in the
egg and stir gently until the
mixture is set. Remove the egg
mixture and set it aside. Heat
another tbsp of the oil and fry
the garlic, shrimp, peas and
scallions quickly for 2 minutes.
Remove from the wok and set
aside. Heat the remaining oil in
the wok and stir in the rice and
remaining salt. Stir-fry to heat the
rice through. Add the egg and
the shrimp mixtures and the soy
sauce, stirring to blend
thoroughly. Serve immediately.

STIR-FRIED RICE WITH PEPPERS

This is a simple vegetable fried rice which goes well with any number of stir-fried meat or fish dishes. The peppers make a crunchy contrast to the rice.

Serves 4

INGREDIENTS

⅔ cup long-grain rice
1 tbsp peanut oil
1 onion, chopped
1 green pepper, de-seeded and
  cut into small pieces
1 red pepper, de-seeded and cut
  into small pieces
1 tbsp soy sauce
Salt and freshly ground black
  pepper
1 tsp sesame oil

Cook the rice in boiling water, then drain and set aside. Heat the oil in a wok and stir-fry the onion. Add the peppers and fry until lightly browned. Add the rice to the wok. Stir in the soy sauce and continue cooking until the rice is heated through completely. Season with salt and pepper and the sesame oil and serve.

SPECIAL FRIED RICE

Special Fried Rice is a meal in itself but it is usually served to accompany a variety of meat or fish dishes. I sometimes serve it with a selection of Chinese vegetables in season.

Serves 4

INGREDIENTS
2 tbsps peanut oil
2 eggs, beaten
Salt and freshly ground black
    pepper
2 scallions, sliced diagonally
1 cup frozen peas
½ pound cooked rice
1 tbsp light soy sauce
1 tbsp dark soy sauce
½ cup beansprouts
½ pound Chinese barbecued
    pork or cooked ham, diced
⅔ cup medium shrimp, shelled
    and de-veined
2 scallion flowers (see recipe for
    Barbecued Spareribs) to
    garnish

Heat a wok and add 1 tbsp of the peanut oil, rolling it around the surface. Make a pancake by mixing the beaten eggs with a pinch of salt and 1 tsp of oil. Pour the egg mixture into the wok, and move the wok about so that the mixture spreads over the surface. When the pancake is lightly browned on the underside, turn it over and cook on the other side. Remove the pancake and set aside to cool.

Heat the remaining oil in the wok. When hot, add the scallions and peas and cook, covered, for 2 minutes. Remove the vegetables with a slotted spoon and set aside. Reheat the oil and add the rice. Stir continuously over low heat until the rice is heated through. Add both soy sauces and mix well. Stir in the peas, scallions, beansprouts, meat, shrimp, and salt and pepper to taste. Mix thoroughly. Serve the rice hot, garnished with shredded pancake and scallion flowers. The pancake may be sliced very finely and mixed into the rice, if preferred.

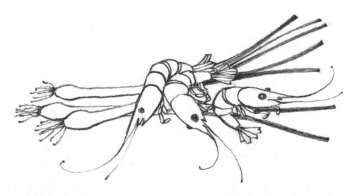

STIR-FRIED STICKY RICE

The Chinese favor a slightly rounded long-grain rice which cooks "sticky" and is therefore much easier to eat with chopsticks than fluffy, separate grains.

Serves 4

INGREDIENTS
1⅓ cups glutinous rice
2 tbsps oil
2 scallions, chopped
½ onion, chopped
1 slice fresh root ginger, peeled
4 Chinese dried black
  mushrooms, soaked for 15
  minutes in warm water, then
  drained and sliced
Salt and freshly ground black
  pepper

Wash the rice in plenty of cold water and place it in a strainer. Pour 5 cups boiling water over the rice. Heat the oil in a wok and fry the scallions, onion and ginger until golden brown. Add the mushrooms and continue cooking, stirring and shaking the wok frequently. Add the rice and stir well, then pour over enough water to cover the rice by ½ inch. Cover and cook over moderate heat until there is almost no liquid left. Lower the heat and continue cooking until all the liquid has been absorbed. This takes approximately 20 minutes in total. Add salt and pepper to taste and serve immediately.

DEEP-FRIED STICKY RICE WITH SHRIMP

Long-grain rice simply will not work for this dish! Use a shorter-grained rice – Thai rice is ideal – that will "cook sticky" and is easy to shape into balls if Chinese glutinous rice cannot be found.

Serves 4

INGREDIENTS

1¼ cups glutinous rice
20 large fresh shrimp
1 tbsp oil
1 tsp finely chopped fresh root ginger
2-3 cloves garlic, chopped
1 small red pepper, de-seeded and finely chopped
1 small green pepper, de-seeded and finely chopped
1 onion, finely chopped
½ cucumber, finely chopped
1 tbsp soy sauce
Juice of 1 orange
2 tsps white wine vinegar
1 tsp sugar
½ cup chicken stock
Salt and freshly ground black pepper
Oil for deep-frying
1 tsp cornstarch, combined with a little water

Steam the rice, then let it dry at room temperature. Shell and de-vein the shrimp. Heat the oil in a large skillet or wok and briefly cook first the ginger and garlic and then the shrimp. Remove with a slotted spoon and set aside. Stir-fry the red and green peppers, onion and cucumber until just cooked. Add the soy sauce, orange juice, vinegar, sugar, chicken stock and salt and pepper to taste. Return the shrimp to the pan and cook over low heat for approximately 10 minutes.

Meanwhile, heat the oil for deep-frying to 340°F. Shape the rice into balls and fry until golden. Drain on paper towels and place in a warm oven. Thicken the shrimp and sauce with the cornstarch, stirring until boiling, and serve the sauce poured over the rice balls.

SINGAPORE FRIED NOODLES

These special fried noodles are a meal in themselves for 2 or 3 people, or may be served with Chinese vegetables in season.

Serves 4

INGREDIENTS

½ pound egg noodles
3 tbsps oil
2 eggs, lightly beaten
Salt and freshly ground black pepper
2 cloves garlic, crushed
1 tsp chili powder
1 boneless chicken breast, skinned and cut into shreds
3 sticks celery, sliced diagonally
2 scallions, sliced
1 red chili, de-seeded and finely sliced
1 green chili, de-seeded and finely sliced
1⅓ cups medium shrimps, shelled and de-veined
½ cup beansprouts
Chili flowers (see recipe for Szechuan Fish) to garnish

Soak the noodles in boiling water for 8 minutes, or as directed on the package. Drain on paper towels and leave to dry.

Heat a wok, and add 1 tbsp of oil. Add the lightly beaten eggs, and salt and pepper to taste. Stir gently and cook until set. Remove the egg from the wok and keep warm.

Add the remaining oil to the wok. When hot, add the garlic and chili powder and fry for 30 seconds. Add the chicken, celery, scallions and red and green chilies, and stir-fry for 8 minutes or until the chicken has cooked through. Finally, add the noodles, shrimp and beansprouts, and toss until well mixed and heated through. Serve with the scrambled egg, broken up with a fork and scattered over the top of the noodles, and garnish with chili flowers.

CRISPY NOODLES

When I was a child we sometimes used to have take-away Chinese meals for a treat on Saturdays, and my favorite dish was always the crispy noodles! Now I know how to make them myself there's no stopping me.

Serves 4 with any stir-fry

INGREDIENTS
1 pound egg noodles
Oil for deep-frying
Salt
Sesame oil

Cook the noodles in plenty of boiling salted water for 12-14 minutes, stirring occasionally. Drain well, and pat dry with paper towels.

Fry the noodles in hot oil for 2-3 minutes until very crispy. Drain well. Sprinkle with salt and sesame oil, then serve immediately.

SOUTH SEA NOODLES

I often choose to eat noodles instead of rice with a Chinese meal. These noodles are almost a meal in themselves but they also go well with plainer meat or vegetable dishes.

Serves 4

INGREDIENTS
2 tbsps Chinese dried shrimp, soaked
½ pound Chinese rice flour vermicelli or fine noodles
¼ cup oil
2 medium onions, sliced
4 strips bacon
2 tbsps curry powder
Salt
⅔ cup chicken stock

Garnish
2 tbsps oil
1⅓ cups shelled medium shrimp
2 cloves garlic, chopped
4 scallions, chopped
1 tbsp soy sauce
1 tbsp Hoisin sauce
1 tbsp pale dry sherry
2 tbsps freshly chopped parsley

Soak the dried shrimp in boiling water for 30 minutes, then drain and chop them. Cook the rice vermicelli in boiling water for 3 minutes, then drain and rinse in cold water.

Heat the oil in a wok, add the onion, bacon and dried shrimp and stir-fry for 1 minute. Add the curry powder and a pinch of salt. Cook for 1 minute, then add the stock and rice vermicelli. Toss well to mix and continue cooking for 2-3 minutes. Transfer the mixture to a heated serving dish.

To prepare the garnish, heat the oil in the wok, add the shrimp and garlic and stir-fry over high heat for 1 minute. Add all the remaining ingredients except the parsely and pour the sauce over the noodles. Sprinkle with the parsley.

PAOTZU STEAMED BUNS WITH PORK, CABBAGE AND MUSHROOMS

These are very light, filled dumplings. The yeast prevents the dumplings from becoming heavy. Add extra flour during kneading if the dough is sticky.

Serves 4

INGREDIENTS
3 cups self-rising flour
1 ounce fresh yeast
1 cup warm water
1 pound cabbage
6 Chinese dried black
    mushrooms, pre-soaked
2 slices fresh root ginger, peeled
½ pound ground pork
1 tbsp salt
1 tbsp soy sauce
1 tsp freshly ground black
    pepper
1 tsp sesame oil

Place the flour in a large bowl. Crumble the yeast into the warm water, stir and leave for 10 minutes or until frothy. Add the yeast liquid to the flour and mix well. Cover and leave in a warm place until doubled in size.

Chop the cabbage, mushrooms and root ginger finely, then place in a bowl and mix with the pork, salt, soy sauce, pepper and sesame oil.

Turn the dough out onto a floured surface and knead until smooth. Divide into pieces 1½ inches in diameter and press a little of the pork filling into each piece, shaping the dough around the filling into round buns. Leave for 15-20 minutes. Place the filled buns in the top of a steamer and steam well for 10-12 minutes. Serve immediately.

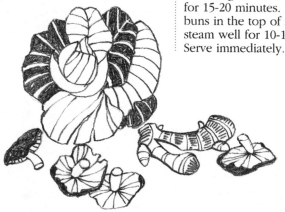

POT STICKER DUMPLINGS

This dish is so called because the dumplings are fried in very little oil. To prevent them from "pot sticking," ensure that they are well browned and crispy on the base before they are steamed.

Serves 4-6

INGREDIENTS
Oil for frying

Dumpling Pastry
1½ cups all-purpose flour
½ tsp salt
3 tbsps oil
Boiling water

Filling
½ pound finely ground pork or
  chicken
4 water chestnuts, finely
  chopped
3 scallions, finely chopped
½ tsp five-spice powder
1 tbsp light soy sauce
1 tsp sugar
1 tsp sesame oil

Sift the flour and salt for the dumpling pastry into a large bowl and make a well in the center. Pour in the oil and add enough boiling water to make a pliable dough. Add about ¼ cup water at first and begin stirring with a wooden spoon to gradually incorporate the flour.

Add more water as necessary. Knead the dough for about 5 minutes and leave to rest for 30 minutes. Divide the dough into 12 pieces and roll each piece out into a circle about 6 inches in diameter.

Mix all the filling ingredients together and place a mound of filling on half of each circle. Fold over the top and press the edges together firmly. Roll the joined edges over using a twisting motion and press down to seal. Pour about ⅛ inch of oil into a large skillet. When the oil is hot, add the dumplings, flat side down, and cook until well browned.

When the underside is brown, add about ⅓ cup water to the pan and cover it tightly. Continue cooking gently for about 5 minutes, or until the top surface of the steamed dumplings looks cooked. Serve immediately.

PEKING ONION PANCAKE

Peking Onion Pancakes are rather like a flour tortilla. They are re-rolled after filling to spread the onion evenly through the pancake. Serve with stir-fried vegetables.

Serves 4

INGREDIENTS
3 cups all-purpose flour
1 cup boiling water
⅓ cup cold water
1 large onion, finely chopped
3 tsps salt
⅓ cup oil

Place the flour in a bowl and gradually add the boiling water, stirring continuously. Leave for 3 minutes, then stir in the cold water and mix into a manageable dough. Turn on to a lightly floured surface and knead well. Cover the dough and leave to rest for 20 minutes.

Divide the dough into 6 pieces and roll each into a 10-inch circle. Sprinkle them with chopped onion and salt, then roll up tightly and twist each pancake into a coil. Press flat with your hand, then roll out until each pancake is ¼ inch thick.

Heat the oil in a large skillet and fry the pancakes for 3 minutes on each side. Keep warm while cooking the remaining pancakes and serve, cut into wedges.

DESSERTS

Desserts are a most unusual concept in the vast majority of Chinese households! There are very few truly classic Chinese dessert recipes and those that do exist have their origins in the Imperial Household, where the time and skills were available to experiment with food. The desserts that I have selected for this chapter show the limited variety of ingredients that are available for sweet dishes. I think that this contributes to the lack of enthusiasm with which Chinese desserts are greeted in the West – they are certainly not as highly regarded as the Chinese savory dishes are. Many desserts are really sweet dim sum, and are still widely served in tea houses.

Most Chinese families would be content to have a piece of fresh fruit to finish a family meal. There are many exotic fruits which, when freshly picked and at the height of their ripeness, would seem to be treasure enough to our Western palates and it is difficult to imagine wanting anything else to conclude a meal. In China a selection of fresh fruits is sometimes served on a bed of ice to keep them very fresh. These are then dipped into sugar before being eaten, making a very simple dessert just a little more special.

Glazed Fruits – a Popular Tradition

One of the desserts which appears most frequently on Chinese restaurants menus (that is, apart from canned lychees and ice cream!) is apple or banana in a crisp sugar coating – the recipe for Sesame Toffee Apples is a delicious variation of this popular dessert. I personally feel that to call this dessert toffee apples confuses it somewhat with the apples that children in the West eat on sticks, but it is the same sort of idea! Sprinkling the fruits with sesame seeds after cooking gives a splendid texture and crunch.

Almonds – a Classic Ingredient in China

There are two types of almonds, sweet and bitter. Both are used in Chinese cooking, either as nuts or as extract or essence and many recipes do call for bitter almond extract. The bitter almonds and bitter almond extract are difficult to obtain in the West and you may have to be content with the regular almonds and their extract, although the resulting flavor of your dessert will not be strictly correct. I have always loved steamed or baked egg custards and sometimes add almond essence to make an alternative flavoring – you could try it with the recipe for Steamed Custard.

Almond tea should not be confused with tea as we drink it or even with green China teas. It is an infusion of ground nuts and rice boiled with water until almost a soup, and is best drunk cold. It can be made into a more traditional dessert by setting it with gelatin or agar-agar, the vegetarian alternative. This is referred to as almond junket, but is not a junket in the true sense of a milk pudding set with rennet.

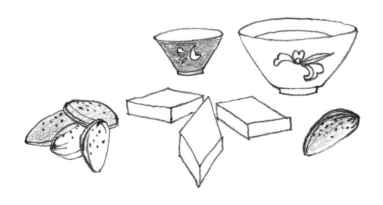

A Treasure Among Puddings

Perhaps the best known of all traditional Chinese desserts is, not surprisingly, a rice pudding! It is the Eight Treasure or Eight Jewel Rice, a molded pudding set in a pan or a pudding basin and coated with a sweet syrup or liqueur before serving; the liqueur, if used, might be heated and flamed. A variety of glacé fruits and nuts is used and sweet bean paste or chestnut purée is spread in layers between the rice as the pudding is made. This dessert is common at banquets and parties in China.

Sweet Wontons – the Perfect Solution

Although desserts are a treat in China, there is a growing addiction to sweet nibbles or dim sum, which may be served almost like a chocolate or a petit four at the end of a meal. These are more common in restaurants than in the home as they are quite demanding in terms of both time and effort to prepare, but they do conclude a meal in a most satisfactory manner. Wontons are a type of dim sum which may easily be prepared at home, using commercially prepared wonton wrappers. Once the folding technique has been mastered, to keep the filling safely enclosed during cooking, the preparation of the wontons is comparatively straightforward. Our recipe is for wontons filled with sweet bean paste, but small fruits or a thick purée – of dates, for example – would also work well. These wontons are fried, drained and then lightly coated with fragrant honey before serving.

STIR-FRIED FRUIT SALAD

*If you are unable to get all the fruits specified here, use a
selection of exotic fruits from the supermarket.*

Serves 4-6

INGREDIENTS
4 slices fresh pineapple
2 Asian pears
1 papaya
1 grapefruit
6 kumquats
½ mango
12 litchis
2 tbsps oil
2 tbsps sugar
Ground cinnamon

Peel and core or de-seed the pineapple, Asian pears and papaya. Cut each into thin slices. Peel the grapefruit and cut into segments. Cut the kumquats into quarters lengthwise or slice crosswise. Remove the pits if wished. Peel the mango, and cut in half either side of the large central stone. Cut the flesh into thin slices. Peel the litchis.

Heat the oil and stir-fry the fruit in the following order: pineapple, litchis, kumquats, mango, Asian pears, papaya and lastly the grapefruit. Sprinkle with the sugar. Cook for a few more minutes then sprinkle with the cinnamon. Serve hot or cold.

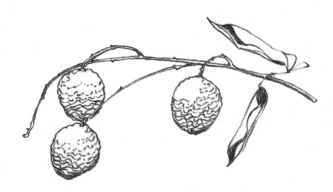

RICE PUDDINGS WITH CRYSTALLIZED FRUIT

These puddings are very sweet and have an unusual, Oriental flavor. Use ordinary almond extract if bitter extract is not available.

Serves 4

INGREDIENTS
1½ cups glutinous rice
¼ cup sugar
½ cup crystallized fruit
2 drops bitter almond extract
20 dates, stoned
1 tsp oil, warmed

Rinse the rice first in cold then in hot water. Place in a saucepan and cover with water to a height of ½ inch above the top of the rice. Bring to a boil and cook, covered, stirring occasionally. Once the rice is almost cooked, remove the pan from the heat – the rice will finish cooking in the hot water.

Stir in the sugar, crystallized fruit and almond extract. Set aside to cool.

Place the dates in a food processor and blend to a smooth, solid paste. Using your fingers, work the paste into 4 flat, even circles to fit 4 greased individual molds or ramekins. (Use the warmed oil for greasing the ramekins.) Place a layer of rice in the base of the ramekins, top with a date circle and finish with another layer of rice. Cover the ramekins and cook in a steamer for 30 minutes to allow the flavors to mix and develop. Let cool and then chill in the refrigerator before serving.

BANANAS COOKED IN COCONUT MILK

Many Chinese desserts are very sweet. This is lighter and less sweet than most, although a fair amount of sweetness does come from the bananas.

Serves 4

INGREDIENTS
1 tbsp brown sugar
1¼ cups flaked coconut
2 cups milk
4-6 large, ripe bananas, peeled and sliced diagonally into 3 or 4 pieces
Flaked coconut, to garnish

Place the sugar, coconut and milk in a wok, and bring just to a boil. Remove from the heat and let cool for 15 minutes, then press the mixture through a strainer or a piece of cheesecloth to squeeze out the juice.

Return the liquid to the wok, and simmer for 10 minutes or until creamy. Add the prepared bananas, and cook slowly until they are soft. Serve immediately, sprinkled with flaked coconut.

STEAMED CUSTARD

*Egg custard is always a treat, and the traditional
Chinese method of cooking it, by steaming, produces very
light results.*

Serves 4

INGREDIENTS
2 cups milk
2 tbps sugar
2 eggs, beaten
¼ tsp vanilla extract
Ground nutmeg or cinnamon

Place the sugar and milk in a wok or large skillet. Heat gently until the milk is just simmering and the sugar has dissolved. Pour into a bowl and leave to cool for 5 minutes. Meanwhile, wash the wok and place a steaming rack inside, with 1½-2 inches of hot water. Return the wok to the heat and bring the water to simmering point.

Pour the milk and sugar mixture over the beaten eggs, beat again, and add the vanilla. Strain the custard into a shallow baking dish and sprinkle lightly with nutmeg or cinnamon. Place on the rack and cover the dish with waxed paper to prevent condensation from dropping into the custard. Cover the wok and steam for 10-15 minutes. Insert the tip of a knife into the center of the custard to test if it is cooked – the blade should come out clean when the custard is set and gelatinous. Cover and cool for 1 hour, then place in the refrigerator until required.

EXOTIC FRUIT SALAD

Always buy exotic fruits a few days before you need them, to let them ripen fully. If they are very hard, leave them in a warm place to ripen. If you cannot obtain all the ones specified, use a selection.

Serves 4

INGREDIENTS
1 papaya
2 kiwi fruits
4 rambutan fruits
4 canned litchis, plus the juice
   from the can
1 pomegranate
3 blood oranges
3 drops bitter almond extract, or
   ordinary almond extract

Peel all the fresh fruit except the pomegranate and the oranges, removing pits as necessary. Try to buy a fully ripe papaya for the salad. Cut it in half and, using a small spoon, remove all the pits and any stringy skin around them. Peel each half, but not too thickly as the flesh immediately below the skin is very good. Finally, cut the flesh into thin slices or other fancy shapes. Peel two of the oranges. Remove all the pith and cut the flesh into segments.

Squeeze the juice from the remaining orange. Mix it with the canned litchi juice and add the almond extract. Cut the kiwi fruit into slices, rounds or small cubes and combine these with the prepared papaya, rambutans, litchis and oranges in a bowl. Prepare the pomegranate by scoring the skin into quarters with a sharp knife. Break the fruit open with your hands and, using a teaspoon, scrape out the seeds. Add to the fruit salad. Pour the almond flavored juices over and leave the salad to marinate for a few hours in the refrigerator. Serve chilled.

KIWI & COCONUT DUO

The green and white color of these fruits is cool and elegant to look at, and the combination of flavors is unusual and refreshing.

Serves 4

INGREDIENTS
4 kiwi fruit
1 fresh coconut
A little sugar (optional)

Remove the ends of the kiwis. Peel them lengthwise with a small sharp knife, then slice them thinly.

Pierce the three "eyes" of the coconut with a screwdriver. Drain out the milk and strain it through cheesecloth. Using a hammer, tap the coconut all around, about a third of the way down the shell from the eyes, until the coconut breaks open. Break the coconut into pieces and cut the coconut flesh into very thin slices. Arrange the kiwi slices on a serving plate and surround them with the slices of coconut. Add a little sugar to the coconut milk, if wished, and pour the milk over the fruit. Serve chilled.

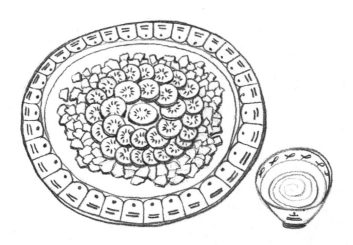

RICE IN MILK

*Chinese Rice Pudding! Dare I suggest that you serve it with a
large spoonful of jam in the middle?*

Serves 4

INGREDIENTS
½ cup long-grain rice
2½ cups milk
1 tbsp clear honey
¼ tsp ground cinnamon
5 cubes sugar

Blanch the rice in boiling water
for 3-4 minutes, rinse well and
set aside to drain. Pour the milk
into a saucepan and stir in the
honey, then sprinkle in the
cinnamon. Stir in the well-
drained rice and the sugar cubes.
Cook over gentle heat, stirring
from time to time. Once the rice
has absorbed all the liquid,
remove it from the heat. Serve
either hot or cold.

STUFFED LITCHIS

This might sound tricky, but it is very easy to pipe a filling into litchis, dates or any small fruit by using a piping bag. A rigid piping tube will not work as well.

Serves 4

INGREDIENTS
10 dates, pitted
2 bananas
Juice ½ lemon
20 canned litchis, reserving a
  little syrup for the sauce

Place the pitted dates in a food processor and blend to a thick paste. Peel and mash the bananas with the lemon juice. Add the date paste and mix together well. Place the mixture in a piping bag and use to stuff the litchis. Mix the litchi syrup into the leftover stuffing to make a sauce. Serve the stuffed chilled litchis with the sauce.

MELON SALAD

A honeydew melon is ideal for this refreshing fruit salad. Fruit salad is the perfect light pudding after a heavy meal of many courses.

Serves 4

INGREDIENTS
1 large honeydew melon
1 mango
4 canned litchis
4 large or 8 small strawberries
Litchi syrup from the can

Peel and seed the melon and cut into thin slices. Peel and pit the mango and cut into thin slices. Using a melon baller, cut as many balls as possible out of the strawberries.

Arrange the melon slices on 4 small plates. Arrange a layer of mango over the melon. Place a litchi in the center of each plate and arrange a few strawberry balls around the edges. Divide the litchi syrup evenly between the plates of fruit and chill them in the refrigerator before serving.

KUMQUATS WITH CRYSTALLIZED GINGER

An Oriental variation on the classic international dessert of oranges in caramel. Kumquats are small tart oranges; a lime variety (limquats) is also available and is equally delicious.

Serves 4

INGREDIENTS
20 kumquats
1-inch piece fresh root ginger, peeled and sliced
1 cup sugar

Use a brush to scrub the kumquats. Blanch them in boiling water and drain, then blanch the root ginger slices and drain. Place the blanched kumquats in a saucepan with the sugar. Cover with water to a height of 2 inches above the fruit. Add the sliced ginger and bring to a boil. Lower the heat and let liquid reduce and caramelize gently. This is a long process, taking about 1½ hours. Add a little more water during cooking, if necessary. Let the dish cool after cooking and then chill in the refrigerator. Cut the ginger into very small pieces before serving.

ALMOND FLOAT WITH FRUIT

Sweet dishes or puddings are seldom served as part of a Chinese meal. There are, however, one or two really special desserts which are suitable for parties and banquets – this is certainly a party dessert.

Serves 6-8

INGREDIENTS
¾ cup water
⅓ cup sugar
1 envelope powdered gelatine
1¼ cups milk
1 tsp almond extract
¼ tsp red or yellow food
  coloring (optional)
Fresh fruit such as kiwi, mango,
  pineapple, bananas, litchis,
  oranges or tangerines, peaches,
  berries, cherries, grapes or
  starfruit
Fresh mint for decoration

Sugar Syrup
⅓ cup sugar
2½ cups water
½ tsp almond extract

Bring the water to a boil in a saucepan and stir in the sugar. Remove the pan from the heat. Sprinkle the gelatin over the water and leave for 1-2 minutes. Stir until the gelatin and sugar dissolve. Add the milk, flavoring and food coloring if used. Mix well and pour into an 8-inch square pan. Chill in the refrigerator until set.

To make the sugar syrup, mix the sugar and water together in a heavy-based pan. Cook over gentle heat until the sugar dissolves, then bring to a boil and let boil for about 2 minutes, or until the syrup thickens slightly. Add the almond extract and let cool to room temperature. Chill in the refrigerator until ready to use. Prepare the fruit and place in attractive serving dish. Pour the chilled syrup over the fruit and mix well. Cut the set almond float into 1-inch diamond shapes or cubes. Use a spatula to remove them from the pan and stir them gently into the fruit mixture. Decorate with sprigs of fresh mint to serve.

EIGHT TREASURE RICE

The Chinese do not generally eat puddings except at banquets and special celebrations. This is one of the most famous puddings – use a pudding basin to cook it in. Use brown dessert dates if jujubes are unavailable.

Serves 6-8

INGREDIENTS

1½ cups pudding rice
¼ cup lard
2 tbsps sugar
15 dried red dates (jujubes), pitted
30 raisins
10 walnut halves
10 glacé cherries
10 pieces of angelica, chopped
8-ounce can sweetened chestnut purée

Syrup
3 tbsps sugar
1¼ cups cold water
1 tbsp cornstarch blended with 2 tbsps water

Place the rice in a saucepan, cover with water and bring to a boil. Lower the heat, cover with a lid and cook for 15 minutes or until the water is absorbed. Add the lard and the sugar to the cooked rice and mix well. Lightly oil a 2½ pint pudding basin and cover the base and sides with a thin layer of the rice mixture. Mix the fruits and nuts together and press into the rice. Spread a second, thicker, layer of rice over the first and fill the center with the chestnut purée. Cover with the remaining rice and flatten the top. Cover with pleated waxed paper and foil and secure with string.

Steam the pudding for 1 hour. Just before it is cooked prepare the syrup. Dissolve the sugar in the water and bring to a boil. Add the cornstarch paste and simmer gently until boiling, thickened and clear. Turn the pudding out onto a heated serving plate and pour the syrup over. Serve immediately, cut into wedge-shaped slices to reveal the layers.

SESAME TOFFEE APPLES

This method may be used to caramelize many fruits but dry fruits, such as apples and bananas, work best. The fruits could be prepared up to the end of their second frying in advance, and the wok cleaned ready for making the caramel. The final stage of cooking is then quick and easy.

Serves 4

INGREDIENTS
2 large, firm apples
5 tbsps all-purpose flour
2 tbsps cornstarch
1 large egg, lightly beaten
1 tsp sesame oil
2 tbsps water
Oil for deep-frying
⅓ cup peanut oil
2 tsps sesame oil
½ cup sugar
2 tbsps white sesame seeds

Peel, core and cut the apples into 1-inch chunks, then toss the apple pieces in 1 tbsp of flour. Mix the rest of the flour with the cornstarch, egg and sesame oil in a small bowl. Mix to a batter with the water and leave for 30 minutes.

Place the oil for deep-frying in a wok, and heat to 350°F. Dip the fruit in batter and coat well.

Deep-fry several pieces at a time until they are golden. Remove from the oil with a slotted spoon and drain on paper towels. Continue cooking in batches until all the fruit is fried. Fry the fruit a second time in the hot oil for 2-3 minutes, then remove with a slotted spoon and drain.

Carefully drain the fat into a bowl to cool, and clean the wok. Fill a bowl with cold water and ice cubes, and put to one side. Place the peanut and sesame oils and the sugar in the wok, and heat until the sugar melts. When it begins to caramelize, stir and add the sesame seeds, then add all the fruit. Toss briefly and gently to coat in the caramel. Take the apple pieces out quickly, and drop them into the ice water a few at a time, to prevent them from sticking together. Serve at once.

PEANUT BUTTER CAKE

Peanut Butter Cake is a popular Oriental dessert. Although light it is surprisingly filling, so only serve small portions.

Serves 4

INGREDIENTS
⅔ cup butter or margarine, softened to room temperature
⅓ cup sugar
4 eggs, separated and the whites stiffly beaten
1 cup all-purpose flour, sifted
Pinch of salt
2 tbsps smooth peanut butter
1 tsp vanilla sugar, or ½ tsp vanilla + 1 tsp sugar
1 tsp grated lemon zest

Lightly grease a shallow 8-inch square baking pan. Beat the softened margarine and sugar together until light and fluffy. Add the egg yolks and beat them in well, then beat in the sifted flour and the salt. Add the peanut butter, vanilla sugar and lemon zest. Beat well to combine all the ingredients. Beat the egg whites in a clean bowl until they form soft peaks. Using a metal spoon or rubber spatula, gently fold in the egg whites, half at a time.

Pour the cake mixture into the baking pan and cook in a 350°F oven for 20-30 minutes, until the cake has risen slightly and is firm to the touch. Let cool before removing from the pan. Serve either slightly warm or chilled.

DATE DUMPLINGS

I would serve these date dumplings with cream or custard
but a canned fruit in syrup, such as mangoes or litchis,
would also be good.

Serves 4

INGREDIENTS
⅔ cup water
⅔ cup milk
2 tsps baking powder
1 tbsp sugar
Pinch of salt
3½ cups all-purpose flour, sifted
15 pitted dates
1 tbsp ground almonds

Mix the water and the milk together, then incorporate the baking powder, sugar and salt. Gradually stir in the flour and cook until the mixture forms a ball. You may find it easier to use your fingers rather than a spoon. Let the dough rest in a warm place for 1 hour.

Place the dates and the almonds in a food processor and blend until a smooth paste is formed. Roll out small lumps of the dough into circles on a lightly floured surface. Place a little of the date mixture in the center of each circle, then pull the edges up over the top, pinching them together well with your fingers to seal. Roll in your hands to form small balls. Steam the dumplings for approximately 20 minutes. You may need to do this in more than one batch. Serve hot or cold.

"HALF-MOON" BANANA PASTRIES

Bananas make a very sweet filling for these pastries. A sauce made with fresh oranges, a little sugar and a sprig or two of mint may not be traditional – but it's very good!

Serves 4

INGREDIENTS

Pastry
4 cups all-purpose flour, sifted
½ cup lard
Pinch of salt
½ cup water

Filling
3 bananas
2 tsps sugar
Pinch cinnamon
¼ tsp lemon juice
1 egg yolk, beaten

Rub the lard into the flour with the salt. Using your fingers, incorporate the water gradually to form a ball. Wrap a damp cloth around the pastry and leave it to rest in a cool place for 30 minutes.

Peel the bananas and mash with a fork in a bowl. Add the sugar, cinnamon and lemon juice and mix well. Roll the pastry out thinly on a lightly floured surface, and cut into circles. Place a little of the banana filling on each circle of pastry and fold into half-moon shapes. Seal the edges first by pinching together with your fingers and then by decorating with a fork. Continue until all the pastry and filling have been used.

Put the half-moon pastries on a baking sheet and brush with the beaten egg yolk. Pierce the pastry once to allow steam to escape during cooking. Bake for approximately 20 minutes in a 350°F oven, until crispy and golden.

SWEET BEAN WONTONS

Wonton wrappers may be stuffed with sweet or savory fillings and are a typical tea house, or café, snack. Sweet red bean paste is available in specialist Chinese food stores.

Serves 6

INGREDIENTS
15 wonton wrappers
½ pound sweet red bean paste
1 tbsp cornstarch
¼ cup cold water
Oil for deep-frying
Honey

Take a wonton wrapper in the palm of your hand and place a little of the red bean paste slightly above the center. Mix the cornstarch and water together and moisten the edge of the wrapper around the filling, then fold over, slightly off center. Pull the sides together, using the cornstarch and water paste to stick the two together, and turn inside out by gently pushing the filled center. The wontons will be similar in shape to tortellini, the filled Italian pasta shapes.

Heat enough oil in a wok for deep-fat frying. When hot, put in four of the filled wontons at a time. Cook until crispy and golden and remove with a slotted spoon, placing the wontons on paper towels to drain. Repeat with the remaining filled wontons. Served trickled with honey.

ALMOND COOKIES

These almond cookies are very like Western-style macaroons.
Let them cool slightly on the baking sheet before transferring
them to a rack to cool completely.

Makes 30 cookies

INGREDIENTS
½ cup butter or margarine
¼ cup superfine sugar
2 tbsps light brown sugar
1 egg, beaten
Almond extract
1 cup all-purpose flour
1 tsp baking powder
Pinch of salt
¼ cup ground almonds,
   blanched or unblanched
30 whole blanched almonds
2 tbsps water

Cream the butter or margarine together with the two sugars until light and fluffy. Divide the beaten egg in half and add half to the sugar mixture with a few drops of the almond extract. Beat until smooth. Reserve the remaining egg for later use. Sift the flour, baking powder and salt into the egg mixture and add the ground almonds. Mix well with your hand. Shape the mixture into small balls with your fingers and place well apart on lightly greased baking sheets. Flatten the balls slightly and press an almond on to the top of each one. Mix the reserved egg with the water and brush each cookie before baking. Bake for 12-15 minutes in a 350°F oven; the cookies will be a pale golden color when done. Cool on a rack.

INDEX

S

Scallops with Asparagus 104

Scrambled Eggs with Crabmeat 93

Sea Bass in Five-spice Sauce 83

Seafood Combination 90

Sesame Chicken Wings 62

Sesame Stir-fry 194

Sesame Toffee Apples 244

Shanghai Long-cooked
  Knuckle of Pork 151

Shark's Fin Soup 33

Shredded Beef with Vegetables 169

Shrimp and Ginger 94

Shrimp Egg Rice 217

Shrimp Toasts 57

Shrimp with Vegetables 96

Singapore Fish 72

Singapore Fried Noodles 222

South Sea Noodles 224

Special Fried Rice 219

Special Mixed Vegetables 191

Spiced Beansprouts with Cucumber
  Shreds 206

Spinach and Radish Salad 205

Spring Rolls 56

Squid with Broccoli and Cauliflower 92

Steamed Cabbage Rolls with Fish
  and Crabmeat 200

Steamed Custard 235

Steamed Fish in Ginger 76

Steamed Fish with Black Beans 73

Steamed Pork with Ground Rice 150

Steamed Sea Bass 87

Steamed Shrimp 100

Steamed Zucchini Flowers 190

Stir-fried Beef with Mango Slices 173

Stir-fried Beef with Oyster Sauce 168

Stir-fried Bok Choy 187

Stir-fried Chicken with
  Sliced Zucchini 121

Stir-fried Chicken with Yellow
  Bean Sauce 115

Stir-fried Fruit Salad 232

Stir-fried Green Beans with Chili 199

Stir-fried Lamb with Sesame Seeds 181

Stir-fried Lobster with Ginger 106

Stir-fried Chicken on Crispy Noodles 112

Stir-fried Pork and Vegetables 159

Stir-fried Rice with Peppers 218

Stir-fried Shrimp and Snow Peas 105

Stir-fried Sliced Pork with Pigs' Liver
  and Kidney 148

Stir-fried Sticky Rice 220

Stir-fried Taro and Carrots 192

Stir-fried Tofu Salad 204

Stuffed Chicken Legs 127

Stuffed Bok Choy 154

Stuffed Litchis 239

Stuffed Snow Peas 189

Sweet Bean Wontons 248

Sweet and Sour Pork 164

Sweet and Sour Shellfish 97

Sweet-sour Fish 74

Szechuan "Yu Hsiang" Pork Ribbons,
  Quick-fried with Shredded Vegetables 147

Szechuan Bang Bang Chicken 110

Szechuan Chili Chicken 111

Szechuan Fish 77

Szechuan Meat Balls 176

T

Ten Varieties of Beauty 197

Triple Fry of "Three Sea Flavors" 99

Trout Fillets with Ginger and Scallion 79

Trout in Oyster Sauce 86

Turkey Soup with Black Mushrooms 43

V

Vegetable Chop Suey 188

W

Whiting Fritters with Cold Fish Sauce 81

Wonton Soup 48

Wonton Soup with Watercress 34

Y

Yangchow Special Fried Rice 216

252